TEACHER'S PET PUBLICATIONS

PUZZLE PACK
for
Oedipus Rex

based on the work by
Sophocles

Written by
Mary B. Collins

© 2007 Teacher's Pet Publications
All Rights Reserved

The materials in this packet are copyrighted
by Teacher's Pet Publications, Inc.

These pages may be duplicated by the purchaser
for use in the purchaser's own classroom.

Copying any of these materials and distributing them
for any other purpose is a violation of the copyright laws.

© 2007 Teacher's Pet Publications, Inc.
www.tpet.com

INTRODUCTION
If you already own the LitPlan for this title, this Puzzle Pack will refresh your Unit Resource Materials and Vocabulary Resource Materials sections plus give you additional materials you can substitute into the tests. If you do not already have a complete LitPlan, these pages will give you some supplemental materials to use with your own plan. There are two main groups of materials: one set for unit words (such as characters' names, symbols, places, etc.) and one set for vocabulary words associated with the book.

WORD LIST
There is a word list for both the unit words and the vocabulary words. These lists show you which words are being used in the materials and the clues or definitions being used for those words. You may want to give students a word list with clues/definitions to help them, or you may want students to only have a word list (without clues/definitions) if you want them to work a little harder. Both are available for duplication. The word lists can also be your "calling key" for the bingo games.

FILL IN THE BLANK AND MATCHING
There are 4 each of the fill in the blank and matching worksheets for both the unit and vocabulary words. These pages can be used either as extra worksheets for students or as objective parts of a unit test. They can be done individually if students need extra help or as a whole class activity to review the material covered.

MAGIC SQUARES
The magic squares not only reinforce the material covered but also work on reasoning and math skills. Many teachers have told us that their students really enjoy doing these!

WORD SEARCH PUZZLES
The word search words go in all directions, as indicated on your answer keys. Two of the word search puzzles have the clues listed rather than the words. This makes the puzzle a little more difficult, but it reinforces the material better. Two word search puzzles have words only for students who find the clue puzzles too difficult.

CROSSWORD PUZZLES
Both unit and vocabulary word sections have 4 crossword puzzles.

BINGO CARDS
There are 32 individual bingo cards for the unit words and 32 individual bingo cards for the vocabulary words. You can use your word list as a "call list," calling the words at random and marking them off of your list as you go, or you could use the flash cards by cutting them apart and drawing the words at random from a hat (or box or whatever). To make a better review, you might ask for the definition and spelling of each word as you call it out–or you could call out the definitions and have students tell you the words they need to look for on the puzzle.

JUGGLE LETTERS
The vocabulary juggle letter game is intended to help students learn the spellings of the words. One sheet has the definitions listed on it as an extra help for students who need it or to reinforce the definitions if you choose to do so.

FLASH CARDS
We've included a set of vocabulary flash cards you can duplicate, cut, and fold for your students. Some teachers make a few sets for general use by the class; others make a set for each student. Some teachers duplicate them for each student and have the students cut & fold their own. You can cut out just the words and put them in a hat, have each student pick out one word and write the definition and a sentence for that word. Students then swap words and papers, with the next student adding a sentence of his own under the last one. You can have students swap as many times as you like. Each time the student will read the sentences written prior to his own and then add a sentence. You can cut out the words and definitions separately and play "I Have; Who Has?" Each student in the room draws a word and definition. The first student says, "I have (the name of the word). Who has the definition?" The student with the definition reads it then says, "I have (the name of the vocabulary word she has). Who has the definition?" The round continues until all words and definitions have been given.

Oedipus Word List

No.	Word	Clue/Definition
1.	ANTIGONE	One of Oedipus's daughters
2.	ANTISTROPHE	Movement of the chorus from left to right across the stage
3.	APOLLO	He is most concerned about Laios's murder.
4.	ATHENA	The Chorus prays to ___. Artemis, & Apollo for help.
5.	BLINDS	Oedipus ___ himself with the brooches from Iocaste's dress.
6.	CATHARSIS	Purification of a character's emotions; an emotional release
7.	CHORAGOS	Leader of the chorus
8.	CORINTH	City in which Oedipus was raised
9.	CREON	He took over as the King of Thebes.
10.	DELPHI	Location of Apollo's temple
11.	DENOUEMENT	Resolution of the main conflict in a play
12.	EPISODE	Scene in a play
13.	EXILE	Oedipus follows his own edict and goes into self-___.
14.	EXODOS	Last song of the play, usually contains a moral lesson
15.	FURIES	They will follow the killer wherever he goes.
16.	HUBRIS	Arrogance demonstrated by a character as a result of pride or passion
17.	IOCASTE	Wife of Laios and Oedipus
18.	KITHAIRON	Infant Oedipus had been left in the shadow of Mt. ___.
19.	LAIOS	King of Thebes who was killed at a place where 3 roads meet
20.	LYING	The Chorus says that Teiresias is ___ in Ode I.
21.	MEROPE	Queen of Corinth feared by Oedipus
22.	ODES	Songs that comment on the action of the play or its characters
23.	OEDIPUS	Killed his father and married his mother
24.	PARODOS	Opening song as the chorus makes its entrance
25.	POLYBOS	King of Corinth who raised the abandoned infant Oedipus
26.	PROLOGUE	Introduces the main characters in the beginning of a play
27.	PROPHECY	A ___ had warned Oedipus of his fate.
28.	RELIEF	Feeling Oedipus has when he hears the King of Corinth is dead
29.	SATYR	Play that comically portrayed mythological stories or poked fun at politics
30.	SHEPHERD	A ___ spared infant Oedipus's life.
31.	SOPHOCLES	Author of Oedipus Rex
32.	SPHINX	Destroyed herself after Oedipus correctly answered her riddle
33.	STROPHE	Movement of the chorus from right to left across the stage
34.	SUICIDE	Iocaste commits this.
35.	TEIRESIAS	Blind prophet
36.	THEBES	City being destroyed by a plague because of an unsolved murder
37.	THESPIS	Father of Greek Theatre
38.	TRAGEDY	Serious play in which the main character suffers from a flaw
39.	TRAITOR	Oedipus accused Creon of being a ___ at the opening of Scene 2 Ode 2.

Oedipus Fill In The Blanks 1

_____ 1. Author of Oedipus Rex

_____ 2. Blind prophet

_____ 3. City in which Oedipus was raised

_____ 4. Destroyed herself after Oedipus correctly answered her riddle

_____ 5. One of Oedipus's daughters

_____ 6. Infant Oedipus had been left in the shadow of Mt. ___.

_____ 7. Resolution of the main conflict in a play

_____ 8. Oedipus follows his own edict and goes into self-___.

_____ 9. Purification of a character's emotions; an emotional release

_____ 10. King of Corinth who raised the abandoned infant Oedipus

_____ 11. City being destroyed by a plague because of an unsolved murder

_____ 12. Location of Apollo's temple

_____ 13. A ___ spared infant Oedipus's life.

_____ 14. Songs that comment on the action of the play or its characters

_____ 15. Serious play in which the main character suffers from a flaw

_____ 16. They will follow the killer wherever he goes.

_____ 17. The Chorus says that Teiresias is ___ in Ode I.

_____ 18. Leader of the chorus

_____ 19. Movement of the chorus from left to right across the stage

_____ 20. He is most concerned about Laios's murder.

Oedipus Fill In The Blanks 1 Answer Key

SOPHOCLES	1. Author of Oedipus Rex
TEIRESIAS	2. Blind prophet
CORINTH	3. City in which Oedipus was raised
SPHINX	4. Destroyed herself after Oedipus correctly answered her riddle
ANTIGONE	5. One of Oedipus's daughters
KITHAIRON	6. Infant Oedipus had been left in the shadow of Mt. ___.
DENOUEMENT	7. Resolution of the main conflict in a play
EXILE	8. Oedipus follows his own edict and goes into self-___.
CATHARSIS	9. Purification of a character's emotions; an emotional release
POLYBOS	10. King of Corinth who raised the abandoned infant Oedipus
THEBES	11. City being destroyed by a plague because of an unsolved murder
DELPHI	12. Location of Apollo's temple
SHEPHERD	13. A ___ spared infant Oedipus's life.
ODES	14. Songs that comment on the action of the play or its characters
TRAGEDY	15. Serious play in which the main character suffers from a flaw
FURIES	16. They will follow the killer wherever he goes.
LYING	17. The Chorus says that Teiresias is ___ in Ode I.
CHORAGOS	18. Leader of the chorus
ANTISTROPHE	19. Movement of the chorus from left to right across the stage
APOLLO	20. He is most concerned about Laios's murder.

Oedipus Fill In The Blanks 2

_____   1. Scene in a play

_____   2. He took over as the King of Thebes.

_____   3. One of Oedipus's daughters

_____   4. Songs that comment on the action of the play or its characters

_____   5. The Chorus prays to ___. Artemis, & Apollo for help.

_____   6. Feeling Oedipus has when he hears the King of Corinth is dead

_____   7. Movement of the chorus from left to right across the stage

_____   8. They will follow the killer wherever he goes.

_____   9. Serious play in which the main character suffers from a flaw

_____   10. He is most concerned about Laios's murder.

_____   11. Leader of the chorus

_____   12. Resolution of the main conflict in a play

_____   13. A ___ had warned Oedipus of his fate.

_____   14. Location of Apollo's temple

_____   15. Destroyed herself after Oedipus correctly answered her riddle

_____   16. Oedipus ___ himself with the brooches from Iocaste's dress.

_____   17. Introduces the main characters in the beginning of a play

_____   18. Wife of Laios and Oedipus

_____   19. Oedipus follows his own edict and goes into self-___.

_____   20. Purification of a character's emotions; an emotional release

Oedipus Fill In The Blanks 2 Answer Key

Answer	Clue
EPISODE	1. Scene in a play
CREON	2. He took over as the King of Thebes.
ANTIGONE	3. One of Oedipus's daughters
ODES	4. Songs that comment on the action of the play or its characters
ATHENA	5. The Chorus prays to ___. Artemis, & Apollo for help.
RELIEF	6. Feeling Oedipus has when he hears the King of Corinth is dead
ANTISTROPHE	7. Movement of the chorus from left to right across the stage
FURIES	8. They will follow the killer wherever he goes.
TRAGEDY	9. Serious play in which the main character suffers from a flaw
APOLLO	10. He is most concerned about Laios's murder.
CHORAGOS	11. Leader of the chorus
DENOUEMENT	12. Resolution of the main conflict in a play
PROPHECY	13. A ___ had warned Oedipus of his fate.
DELPHI	14. Location of Apollo's temple
SPHINX	15. Destroyed herself after Oedipus correctly answered her riddle
BLINDS	16. Oedipus ___ himself with the brooches from Iocaste's dress.
PROLOGUE	17. Introduces the main characters in the beginning of a play
IOCASTE	18. Wife of Laios and Oedipus
EXILE	19. Oedipus follows his own edict and goes into self-___.
CATHARSIS	20. Purification of a character's emotions; an emotional release

Copyrighted

Oedipus Fill In The Blanks 3

_____ 1. King of Corinth who raised the abandoned infant Oedipus

_____ 2. Wife of Laios and Oedipus

_____ 3. The Chorus prays to ___. Artemis, & Apollo for help.

_____ 4. Killed his father and married his mother

_____ 5. King of Thebes who was killed at a place where 3 roads meet

_____ 6. Author of Oedipus Rex

_____ 7. They will follow the killer wherever he goes.

_____ 8. Oedipus ___ himself with the brooches from Iocaste's dress.

_____ 9. City in which Oedipus was raised

_____ 10. City being destroyed by a plague because of an unsolved murder

_____ 11. Infant Oedipus had been left in the shadow of Mt. ___.

_____ 12. Oedipus follows his own edict and goes into self-___.

_____ 13. Feeling Oedipus has when he hears the King of Corinth is dead

_____ 14. Queen of Corinth feared by Oedipus

_____ 15. A ___ spared infant Oedipus's life.

_____ 16. Iocaste commits this.

_____ 17. A ___ had warned Oedipus of his fate.

_____ 18. Oedipus accused Creon of being a ___ at the opening of Scene 2 Ode 2.

_____ 19. Location of Apollo's temple

_____ 20. Blind prophet

Oedipus Fill In The Blanks 3 Answer Key

POLYBOS	1. King of Corinth who raised the abandoned infant Oedipus
IOCASTE	2. Wife of Laios and Oedipus
ATHENA	3. The Chorus prays to ___. Artemis, & Apollo for help.
OEDIPUS	4. Killed his father and married his mother
LAIOS	5. King of Thebes who was killed at a place where 3 roads meet
SOPHOCLES	6. Author of Oedipus Rex
FURIES	7. They will follow the killer wherever he goes.
BLINDS	8. Oedipus ___ himself with the brooches from Iocaste's dress.
CORINTH	9. City in which Oedipus was raised
THEBES	10. City being destroyed by a plague because of an unsolved murder
KITHAIRON	11. Infant Oedipus had been left in the shadow of Mt. ___.
EXILE	12. Oedipus follows his own edict and goes into self-___.
RELIEF	13. Feeling Oedipus has when he hears the King of Corinth is dead
MEROPE	14. Queen of Corinth feared by Oedipus
SHEPHERD	15. A ___ spared infant Oedipus's life.
SUICIDE	16. Iocaste commits this.
PROPHECY	17. A ___ had warned Oedipus of his fate.
TRAITOR	18. Oedipus accused Creon of being a ___ at the opening of Scene 2 Ode 2.
DELPHI	19. Location of Apollo's temple
TEIRESIAS	20. Blind prophet

Oedipus Fill In The Blanks 4

_____

_____

_____

_____

_____

_____

_____

_____

_____

_____

_____

_____

_____

_____

_____

_____

_____

_____

_____

_____

1. A ___ had warned Oedipus of his fate.
2. Queen of Corinth feared by Oedipus
3. A ___ spared infant Oedipus's life.
4. Oedipus accused Creon of being a ___ at the opening of Scene 2 Ode 2.
5. The Chorus prays to ___. Artemis, & Apollo for help.
6. Oedipus ___ himself with the brooches from Iocaste's dress.
7. Blind prophet
8. Feeling Oedipus has when he hears the King of Corinth is dead
9. The Chorus says that Teiresias is ___ in Ode I.
10. Iocaste commits this.
11. City being destroyed by a plague because of an unsolved murder
12. Oedipus follows his own edict and goes into self-___.
13. Location of Apollo's temple
14. King of Corinth who raised the abandoned infant Oedipus
15. Author of Oedipus Rex
16. He is most concerned about Laios's murder.
17. He took over as the King of Thebes.
18. Destroyed herself after Oedipus correctly answered her riddle
19. King of Thebes who was killed at a place where 3 roads meet
20. Wife of Laios and Oedipus

Oedipus Fill In The Blanks 4 Answer Key

PROPHECY	1. A ___ had warned Oedipus of his fate.
MEROPE	2. Queen of Corinth feared by Oedipus
SHEPHERD	3. A ___ spared infant Oedipus's life.
TRAITOR	4. Oedipus accused Creon of being a ___ at the opening of Scene 2 Ode 2.
ATHENA	5. The Chorus prays to ___. Artemis, & Apollo for help.
BLINDS	6. Oedipus ___ himself with the brooches from Iocaste's dress.
TEIRESIAS	7. Blind prophet
RELIEF	8. Feeling Oedipus has when he hears the King of Corinth is dead
LYING	9. The Chorus says that Teiresias is ___ in Ode I.
SUICIDE	10. Iocaste commits this.
THEBES	11. City being destroyed by a plague because of an unsolved murder
EXILE	12. Oedipus follows his own edict and goes into self-___.
DELPHI	13. Location of Apollo's temple
POLYBOS	14. King of Corinth who raised the abandoned infant Oedipus
SOPHOCLES	15. Author of Oedipus Rex
APOLLO	16. He is most concerned about Laios's murder.
CREON	17. He took over as the King of Thebes.
SPHINX	18. Destroyed herself after Oedipus correctly answered her riddle
LAIOS	19. King of Thebes who was killed at a place where 3 roads meet
IOCASTE	20. Wife of Laios and Oedipus

Oedipus Matching 1

___ 1. MEROPE   A. Killed his father and married his mother
___ 2. EXODOS   B. King of Thebes who was killed at a place where 3 roads meet
___ 3. THESPIS   C. He took over as the King of Thebes.
___ 4. DELPHI   D. Infant Oedipus had been left in the shadow of Mt. ___.
___ 5. BLINDS   E. Iocaste commits this.
___ 6. FURIES   F. One of Oedipus's daughters
___ 7. SOPHOCLES   G. City being destroyed by a plague because of an unsolved murder
___ 8. ATHENA   H. Introduces the main characters in the beginning of a play
___ 9. THEBES   I. He is most concerned about Laios's murder.
___10. OEDIPUS   J. Play that comically portrayed mythological stories or poked fun at politics
___11. EXILE   K. Father of Greek Theatre
___12. LYING   L. Author of Oedipus Rex
___13. STROPHE   M. Destroyed herself after Oedipus correctly answered her riddle
___14. CORINTH   N. Oedipus accused Creon of being a ___ at the opening of Scene 2 Ode 2.
___15. SATYR   O. Oedipus follows his own edict and goes into self-___.
___16. PROLOGUE   P. The Chorus says that Teiresias is ___ in Ode I.
___17. TRAITOR   Q. Location of Apollo's temple
___18. SPHINX   R. Songs that comment on the action of the play or its characters
___19. ODES   S. The Chorus prays to ___. Artemis, & Apollo for help.
___20. APOLLO   T. Last song of the play, usually contains a moral lesson
___21. LAIOS   U. Queen of Corinth feared by Oedipus
___22. CREON   V. City in which Oedipus was raised
___23. ANTIGONE   W. Movement of the chorus from right to left across the stage
___24. SUICIDE   X. They will follow the killer wherever he goes.
___25. KITHAIRON   Y. Oedipus ___ himself with the brooches from Iocaste's dress.

Oedipus Matching 1 Answer Key

U - 1. MEROPE	A. Killed his father and married his mother
T - 2. EXODOS	B. King of Thebes who was killed at a place where 3 roads meet
K - 3. THESPIS	C. He took over as the King of Thebes.
Q - 4. DELPHI	D. Infant Oedipus had been left in the shadow of Mt. ___.
Y - 5. BLINDS	E. Iocaste commits this.
X - 6. FURIES	F. One of Oedipus's daughters
L - 7. SOPHOCLES	G. City being destroyed by a plague because of an unsolved murder
S - 8. ATHENA	H. Introduces the main characters in the beginning of a play
G - 9. THEBES	I. He is most concerned about Laios's murder.
A - 10. OEDIPUS	J. Play that comically portrayed mythological stories or poked fun at politics
O - 11. EXILE	K. Father of Greek Theatre
P - 12. LYING	L. Author of Oedipus Rex
W - 13. STROPHE	M. Destroyed herself after Oedipus correctly answered her riddle
V - 14. CORINTH	N. Oedipus accused Creon of being a ___ at the opening of Scene 2 Ode 2.
J - 15. SATYR	O. Oedipus follows his own edict and goes into self-___.
H - 16. PROLOGUE	P. The Chorus says that Teiresias is ___ in Ode I.
N - 17. TRAITOR	Q. Location of Apollo's temple
M - 18. SPHINX	R. Songs that comment on the action of the play or its characters
R - 19. ODES	S. The Chorus prays to ___, Artemis, & Apollo for help.
I - 20. APOLLO	T. Last song of the play, usually contains a moral lesson
B - 21. LAIOS	U. Queen of Corinth feared by Oedipus
C - 22. CREON	V. City in which Oedipus was raised
F - 23. ANTIGONE	W. Movement of the chorus from right to left across the stage
E - 24. SUICIDE	X. They will follow the killer wherever he goes.
D - 25. KITHAIRON	Y. Oedipus ___ himself with the brooches from Iocaste's dress.

Oedipus Matching 2

___ 1. CHORAGOS   A. Infant Oedipus had been left in the shadow of Mt. ___.
___ 2. STROPHE   B. Resolution of the main conflict in a play
___ 3. BLINDS   C. He took over as the King of Thebes.
___ 4. LYING   D. Songs that comment on the action of the play or its characters
___ 5. THESPIS   E. King of Corinth who raised the abandoned infant Oedipus
___ 6. APOLLO   F. A ___ spared infant Oedipus's life.
___ 7. RELIEF   G. King of Thebes who was killed at a place where 3 roads meet
___ 8. SPHINX   H. Father of Greek Theatre
___ 9. CORINTH   I. Wife of Laios and Oedipus
___ 10. KITHAIRON   J. Destroyed herself after Oedipus correctly answered her riddle
___ 11. IOCASTE   K. He is most concerned about Laios's murder.
___ 12. EPISODE   L. The Chorus prays to ___, Artemis, & Apollo for help.
___ 13. ANTIGONE   M. Feeling Oedipus has when he hears the King of Corinth is dead
___ 14. POLYBOS   N. Queen of Corinth feared by Oedipus
___ 15. THEBES   O. Oedipus ___ himself with the brooches from Iocaste's dress.
___ 16. FURIES   P. City being destroyed by a plague because of an unsolved murder
___ 17. ATHENA   Q. The Chorus says that Teiresias is ___ in Ode I.
___ 18. SUICIDE   R. Iocaste commits this.
___ 19. LAIOS   S. Leader of the chorus
___ 20. MEROPE   T. Scene in a play
___ 21. DENOUEMENT   U. One of Oedipus's daughters
___ 22. SHEPHERD   V. They will follow the killer wherever he goes.
___ 23. ODES   W. Introduces the main characters in the beginning of a play
___ 24. PROLOGUE   X. Movement of the chorus from right to left across the stage
___ 25. CREON   Y. City in which Oedipus was raised

Oedipus Matching 2 Answer Key

S - 1. CHORAGOS		A. Infant Oedipus had been left in the shadow of Mt. ___.
X - 2. STROPHE		B. Resolution of the main conflict in a play
O - 3. BLINDS		C. He took over as the King of Thebes.
Q - 4. LYING		D. Songs that comment on the action of the play or its characters
H - 5. THESPIS		E. King of Corinth who raised the abandoned infant Oedipus
K - 6. APOLLO		F. A ___ spared infant Oedipus's life.
M - 7. RELIEF		G. King of Thebes who was killed at a place where 3 roads meet
J - 8. SPHINX		H. Father of Greek Theatre
Y - 9. CORINTH		I. Wife of Laios and Oedipus
A - 10. KITHAIRON		J. Destroyed herself after Oedipus correctly answered her riddle
I - 11. IOCASTE		K. He is most concerned about Laios's murder.
T - 12. EPISODE		L. The Chorus prays to ___. Artemis, & Apollo for help.
U - 13. ANTIGONE		M. Feeling Oedipus has when he hears the King of Corinth is dead
E - 14. POLYBOS		N. Queen of Corinth feared by Oedipus
P - 15. THEBES		O. Oedipus ___ himself with the brooches from Iocaste's dress.
V - 16. FURIES		P. City being destroyed by a plague because of an unsolved murder
L - 17. ATHENA		Q. The Chorus says that Teiresias is ___ in Ode I.
R - 18. SUICIDE		R. Iocaste commits this.
G - 19. LAIOS		S. Leader of the chorus
N - 20. MEROPE		T. Scene in a play
B - 21. DENOUEMENT		U. One of Oedipus's daughters
F - 22. SHEPHERD		V. They will follow the killer wherever he goes.
D - 23. ODES		W. Introduces the main characters in the beginning of a play
W - 24. PROLOGUE		X. Movement of the chorus from right to left across the stage
C - 25. CREON		Y. City in which Oedipus was raised

Oedipus Matching 3

___ 1. SPHINX   A. A ___ spared infant Oedipus's life.
___ 2. MEROPE   B. Blind prophet
___ 3. TRAITOR   C. Queen of Corinth feared by Oedipus
___ 4. POLYBOS   D. Feeling Oedipus has when he hears the King of Corinth is dead
___ 5. THEBES   E. The Chorus says that Teiresias is ___ in Ode I.
___ 6. TEIRESIAS   F. Killed his father and married his mother
___ 7. CORINTH   G. King of Corinth who raised the abandoned infant Oedipus
___ 8. EXILE   H. Author of Oedipus Rex
___ 9. KITHAIRON   I. King of Thebes who was killed at a place where 3 roads meet
___10. IOCASTE   J. Oedipus ___ himself with the brooches from Iocaste's dress.
___11. ATHENA   K. Iocaste commits this.
___12. LYING   L. Infant Oedipus had been left in the shadow of Mt. ___.
___13. OEDIPUS   M. The Chorus prays to ___. Artemis, & Apollo for help.
___14. FURIES   N. Wife of Laios and Oedipus
___15. RELIEF   O. Oedipus accused Creon of being a ___ at the opening of Scene 2 Ode 2.
___16. PROPHECY   P. Location of Apollo's temple
___17. BLINDS   Q. City being destroyed by a plague because of an unsolved murder
___18. SOPHOCLES   R. He is most concerned about Laios's murder.
___19. APOLLO   S. They will follow the killer wherever he goes.
___20. SUICIDE   T. City in which Oedipus was raised
___21. DELPHI   U. Destroyed herself after Oedipus correctly answered her riddle
___22. ANTIGONE   V. He took over as the King of Thebes.
___23. SHEPHERD   W. Oedipus follows his own edict and goes into self-___.
___24. LAIOS   X. A ___ had warned Oedipus of his fate.
___25. CREON   Y. One of Oedipus's daughters

Oedipus Matching 3 Answer Key

U - 1. SPHINX	A.	A ___ spared infant Oedipus's life.
C - 2. MEROPE	B.	Blind prophet
O - 3. TRAITOR	C.	Queen of Corinth feared by Oedipus
G - 4. POLYBOS	D.	Feeling Oedipus has when he hears the King of Corinth is dead
Q - 5. THEBES	E.	The Chorus says that Teiresias is ___ in Ode I.
B - 6. TEIRESIAS	F.	Killed his father and married his mother
T - 7. CORINTH	G.	King of Corinth who raised the abandoned infant Oedipus
W - 8. EXILE	H.	Author of Oedipus Rex
L - 9. KITHAIRON	I.	King of Thebes who was killed at a place where 3 roads meet
N - 10. IOCASTE	J.	Oedipus ___ himself with the brooches from Iocaste's dress.
M - 11. ATHENA	K.	Iocaste commits this.
E - 12. LYING	L.	Infant Oedipus had been left in the shadow of Mt. ___.
F - 13. OEDIPUS	M.	The Chorus prays to ___. Artemis, & Apollo for help.
S - 14. FURIES	N.	Wife of Laios and Oedipus
D - 15. RELIEF	O.	Oedipus accused Creon of being a ___ at the opening of Scene 2 Ode 2.
X - 16. PROPHECY	P.	Location of Apollo's temple
J - 17. BLINDS	Q.	City being destroyed by a plague because of an unsolved murder
H - 18. SOPHOCLES	R.	He is most concerned about Laios's murder.
R - 19. APOLLO	S.	They will follow the killer wherever he goes.
K - 20. SUICIDE	T.	City in which Oedipus was raised
P - 21. DELPHI	U.	Destroyed herself after Oedipus correctly answered her riddle
Y - 22. ANTIGONE	V.	He took over as the King of Thebes.
A - 23. SHEPHERD	W.	Oedipus follows his own edict and goes into self-___.
I - 24. LAIOS	X.	A ___ had warned Oedipus of his fate.
V - 25. CREON	Y.	One of Oedipus's daughters

Oedipus Matching 4

___ 1. KITHAIRON   A. Infant Oedipus had been left in the shadow of Mt. ___.
___ 2. RELIEF   B. City in which Oedipus was raised
___ 3. FURIES   C. Oedipus follows his own edict and goes into self-___.
___ 4. LYING   D. Feeling Oedipus has when he hears the King of Corinth is dead
___ 5. DELPHI   E. The Chorus prays to ___. Artemis, & Apollo for help.
___ 6. ANTIGONE   F. Iocaste commits this.
___ 7. ATHENA   G. He took over as the King of Thebes.
___ 8. SHEPHERD   H. Destroyed herself after Oedipus correctly answered her riddle
___ 9. BLINDS   I. The Chorus says that Teiresias is ___ in Ode I.
___10. SUICIDE   J. King of Thebes who was killed at a place where 3 roads meet
___11. OEDIPUS   K. A ___ spared infant Oedipus's life.
___12. LAIOS   L. He is most concerned about Laios's murder.
___13. MEROPE   M. Author of Oedipus Rex
___14. PROPHECY   N. Blind prophet
___15. TEIRESIAS   O. City being destroyed by a plague because of an unsolved murder
___16. TRAITOR   P. Wife of Laios and Oedipus
___17. CORINTH   Q. Oedipus accused Creon of being a ___ at the opening of Scene 2 Ode 2.
___18. CREON   R. Queen of Corinth feared by Oedipus
___19. POLYBOS   S. One of Oedipus's daughters
___20. SOPHOCLES   T. A ___ had warned Oedipus of his fate.
___21. IOCASTE   U. Location of Apollo's temple
___22. SPHINX   V. King of Corinth who raised the abandoned infant Oedipus
___23. THEBES   W. Oedipus ___ himself with the brooches from Iocaste's dress.
___24. APOLLO   X. They will follow the killer wherever he goes.
___25. EXILE   Y. Killed his father and married his mother

Oedipus Matching 4 Answer Key

A - 1. KITHAIRON	A.	Infant Oedipus had been left in the shadow of Mt. ___.
D - 2. RELIEF	B.	City in which Oedipus was raised
X - 3. FURIES	C.	Oedipus follows his own edict and goes into self-___.
I - 4. LYING	D.	Feeling Oedipus has when he hears the King of Corinth is dead
U - 5. DELPHI	E.	The Chorus prays to ___. Artemis, & Apollo for help.
S - 6. ANTIGONE	F.	Iocaste commits this.
E - 7. ATHENA	G.	He took over as the King of Thebes.
K - 8. SHEPHERD	H.	Destroyed herself after Oedipus correctly answered her riddle
W - 9. BLINDS	I.	The Chorus says that Teiresias is ___ in Ode I.
F - 10. SUICIDE	J.	King of Thebes who was killed at a place where 3 roads meet
Y - 11. OEDIPUS	K.	A ___ spared infant Oedipus's life.
J - 12. LAIOS	L.	He is most concerned about Laios's murder.
R - 13. MEROPE	M.	Author of Oedipus Rex
T - 14. PROPHECY	N.	Blind prophet
N - 15. TEIRESIAS	O.	City being destroyed by a plague because of an unsolved murder
Q - 16. TRAITOR	P.	Wife of Laios and Oedipus
B - 17. CORINTH	Q.	Oedipus accused Creon of being a ___ at the opening of Scene 2 Ode 2.
G - 18. CREON	R.	Queen of Corinth feared by Oedipus
V - 19. POLYBOS	S.	One of Oedipus's daughters
M - 20. SOPHOCLES	T.	A ___ had warned Oedipus of his fate.
P - 21. IOCASTE	U.	Location of Apollo's temple
H - 22. SPHINX	V.	King of Corinth who raised the abandoned infant Oedipus
O - 23. THEBES	W.	Oedipus ___ himself with the brooches from Iocaste's dress.
L - 24. APOLLO	X.	They will follow the killer wherever he goes.
C - 25. EXILE	Y.	Killed his father and married his mother

Oedipus Magic Squares 1

Match the definition with the vocabulary word. Put your answers in the magic squares below. When your answers are correct, all columns and rows will add to the same number.

A. THESPIS   E. IOCASTE   I. LYING   M. RELIEF
B. STROPHE   F. POLYBOS   J. APOLLO   N. EXODOS
C. HUBRIS   G. PROLOGUE   K. THEBES   O. CREON
D. ANTISTROPHE   H. EPISODE   L. OEDIPUS   P. PROPHECY

1. Scene in a play
2. Father of Greek Theatre
3. Movement of the chorus from right to left across the stage
4. Introduces the main characters in the beginning of a play
5. He is most concerned about Laios's murder.
6. He took over as the King of Thebes.
7. A ___ had warned Oedipus of his fate.
8. The Chorus says that Teiresias is ___ in Ode I.
9. City being destroyed by a plague because of an unsolved murder
10. Last song of the play, usually contains a moral lesson
11. Feeling Oedipus has when he hears the King of Corinth is dead
12. Killed his father and married his mother
13. Wife of Laios and Oedipus
14. Movement of the chorus from left to right across the stage
15. Arrogance demonstrated by a character as a result of pride or passion
16. King of Corinth who raised the abandoned infant Oedipus

A=	B=	C=	D=
E=	F=	G=	H=
I=	J=	K=	L=
M=	N=	O=	P=

Oedipus Magic Squares 1 Answer Key

Match the definition with the vocabulary word. Put your answers in the magic squares below. When your answers are correct, all columns and rows will add to the same number.

A. THESPIS
B. STROPHE
C. HUBRIS
D. ANTISTROPHE
E. IOCASTE
F. POLYBOS
G. PROLOGUE
H. EPISODE
I. LYING
J. APOLLO
K. THEBES
L. OEDIPUS
M. RELIEF
N. EXODOS
O. CREON
P. PROPHECY

1. Scene in a play
2. Father of Greek Theatre
3. Movement of the chorus from right to left across the stage
4. Introduces the main characters in the beginning of a play
5. He is most concerned about Laios's murder.
6. He took over as the King of Thebes.
7. A ___ had warned Oedipus of his fate.
8. The Chorus says that Teiresias is ___ in Ode I.
9. City being destroyed by a plague because of an unsolved murder
10. Last song of the play, usually contains a moral lesson
11. Feeling Oedipus has when he hears the King of Corinth is dead
12. Killed his father and married his mother
13. Wife of Laios and Oedipus
14. Movement of the chorus from left to right across the stage
15. Arrogance demonstrated by a character as a result of pride or passion
16. King of Corinth who raised the abandoned infant Oedipus

A=2	B=3	C=15	D=14
E=13	F=16	G=4	H=1
I=8	J=5	K=9	L=12
M=11	N=10	O=6	P=7

Oedipus Magic Squares 2

Match the definition with the vocabulary word. Put your answers in the magic squares below. When your answers are correct, all columns and rows will add to the same number.

A. THESPIS E. CREON   I. OEDIPUS   M. DENOUEMENT
B. PROPHECY F. BLINDS   J. RELIEF   N. THEBES
C. FURIES   G. PROLOGUE   K. SPHINX   O. SUICIDE
D. CHORAGOS H. EPISODE   L. APOLLO   P. TRAITOR

1. Scene in a play
2. Resolution of the main conflict in a play
3. A ___ had warned Oedipus of his fate.
4. Destroyed herself after Oedipus correctly answered her riddle
5. Feeling Oedipus has when he hears the King of Corinth is dead
6. They will follow the killer wherever he goes.
7. Oedipus accused Creon of being a ___ at the opening of Scene 2 Ode 2.
8. He took over as the King of Thebes.
9. Iocaste commits this.
10. Oedipus ___ himself with the brooches from Iocaste's dress.
11. Killed his father and married his mother
12. Leader of the chorus
13. Father of Greek Theatre
14. He is most concerned about Laios's murder.
15. Introduces the main characters in the beginning of a play
16. City being destroyed by a plague because of an unsolved murder

A=	B=	C=	D=
E=	F=	G=	H=
I=	J=	K=	L=
M=	N=	O=	P=

Oedipus Magic Squares 2 Answer Key

Match the definition with the vocabulary word. Put your answers in the magic squares below. When your answers are correct, all columns and rows will add to the same number.

A. THESPIS E. CREON I. OEDIPUS M. DENOUEMENT
B. PROPHECY F. BLINDS J. RELIEF N. THEBES
C. FURIES G. PROLOGUE K. SPHINX O. SUICIDE
D. CHORAGOS H. EPISODE L. APOLLO P. TRAITOR

1. Scene in a play
2. Resolution of the main conflict in a play
3. A ___ had warned Oedipus of his fate.
4. Destroyed herself after Oedipus correctly answered her riddle
5. Feeling Oedipus has when he hears the King of Corinth is dead
6. They will follow the killer wherever he goes.
7. Oedipus accused Creon of being a ___ at the opening of Scene 2 Ode 2.
8. He took over as the King of Thebes.
9. Iocaste commits this.
10. Oedipus ___ himself with the brooches from Iocaste's dress.
11. Killed his father and married his mother
12. Leader of the chorus
13. Father of Greek Theatre
14. He is most concerned about Laios's murder.
15. Introduces the main characters in the beginning of a play
16. City being destroyed by a plague because of an unsolved murder

A=13	B=3	C=6	D=12
E=8	F=10	G=15	H=1
I=11	J=5	K=4	L=14
M=2	N=16	O=9	P=7

Oedipus Magic Squares 3

Match the definition with the vocabulary word. Put your answers in the magic squares below. When your answers are correct, all columns and rows will add to the same number.

A. CORINTH   E. ANTIGONE   I. CREON   M. RELIEF
B. BLINDS   F. PROPHECY   J. IOCASTE   N. APOLLO
C. SOPHOCLES   G. KITHAIRON   K. FURIES   O. SPHINX
D. DELPHI   H. LAIOS   L. LYING   P. POLYBOS

1. City in which Oedipus was raised
2. He is most concerned about Laios's murder.
3. Wife of Laios and Oedipus
4. One of Oedipus's daughters
5. Infant Oedipus had been left in the shadow of Mt. ___.
6. The Chorus says that Teiresias is ___ in Ode I.
7. King of Corinth who raised the abandoned infant Oedipus
8. Author of Oedipus Rex
9. Destroyed herself after Oedipus correctly answered her riddle
10. Location of Apollo's temple
11. King of Thebes who was killed at a place where 3 roads meet
12. They will follow the killer wherever he goes.
13. He took over as the King of Thebes.
14. A ___ had warned Oedipus of his fate.
15. Oedipus ___ himself with the brooches from Iocaste's dress.
16. Feeling Oedipus has when he hears the King of Corinth is dead

A=	B=	C=	D=
E=	F=	G=	H=
I=	J=	K=	L=
M=	N=	O=	P=

Oedipus Magic Squares 3 Answer Key

Match the definition with the vocabulary word. Put your answers in the magic squares below. When your answers are correct, all columns and rows will add to the same number.

A. CORINTH   E. ANTIGONE   I. CREON   M. RELIEF
B. BLINDS   F. PROPHECY   J. IOCASTE   N. APOLLO
C. SOPHOCLES   G. KITHAIRON   K. FURIES   O. SPHINX
D. DELPHI   H. LAIOS   L. LYING   P. POLYBOS

1. City in which Oedipus was raised
2. He is most concerned about Laios's murder.
3. Wife of Laios and Oedipus
4. One of Oedipus's daughters
5. Infant Oedipus had been left in the shadow of Mt. ___.
6. The Chorus says that Teiresias is ___ in Ode I.
7. King of Corinth who raised the abandoned infant Oedipus
8. Author of Oedipus Rex
9. Destroyed herself after Oedipus correctly answered her riddle
10. Location of Apollo's temple
11. King of Thebes who was killed at a place where 3 roads meet
12. They will follow the killer wherever he goes.
13. He took over as the King of Thebes.
14. A ___ had warned Oedipus of his fate.
15. Oedipus ___ himself with the brooches from Iocaste's dress.
16. Feeling Oedipus has when he hears the King of Corinth is dead

A=1	B=15	C=8	D=10
E=4	F=14	G=5	H=11
I=13	J=3	K=12	L=6
M=16	N=2	O=9	P=7

Oedipus Magic Squares 4

Match the definition with the vocabulary word. Put your answers in the magic squares below. When your answers are correct, all columns and rows will add to the same number.

A. SOPHOCLES   E. TRAITOR   I. OEDIPUS   M. SHEPHERD
B. ATHENA   F. LYING   J. IOCASTE   N. KITHAIRON
C. BLINDS   G. CORINTH   K. FURIES   O. LAIOS
D. CREON   H. THEBES   L. PROPHECY   P. POLYBOS

1. King of Thebes who was killed at a place where 3 roads meet
2. He took over as the King of Thebes.
3. Wife of Laios and Oedipus
4. Oedipus accused Creon of being a ___ at the opening of Scene 2 Ode 2.
5. Killed his father and married his mother
6. The Chorus says that Teiresias is ___ in Ode I.
7. King of Corinth who raised the abandoned infant Oedipus
8. Oedipus ___ himself with the brooches from Iocaste's dress.
9. City being destroyed by a plague because of an unsolved murder
10. They will follow the killer wherever he goes.
11. Author of Oedipus Rex
12. Infant Oedipus had been left in the shadow of Mt. ___.
13. The Chorus prays to ___, Artemis, & Apollo for help.
14. A ___ spared infant Oedipus's life.
15. City in which Oedipus was raised
16. A ___ had warned Oedipus of his fate.

A= 11	B= 13	C= 8	D= 2
E= 4	F= 6	G= 15	H= 9
I= 5	J= 3	K= 10	L= 16
M= 14	N= 12	O= 1	P= 7

Oedipus Magic Squares 4 Answer Key

Match the definition with the vocabulary word. Put your answers in the magic squares below. When your answers are correct, all columns and rows will add to the same number.

A. SOPHOCLES   E. TRAITOR   I. OEDIPUS   M. SHEPHERD
B. ATHENA   F. LYING   J. IOCASTE   N. KITHAIRON
C. BLINDS   G. CORINTH   K. FURIES   O. LAIOS
D. CREON   H. THEBES   L. PROPHECY   P. POLYBOS

1. King of Thebes who was killed at a place where 3 roads meet
2. He took over as the King of Thebes.
3. Wife of Laios and Oedipus
4. Oedipus accused Creon of being a ___ at the opening of Scene 2 Ode 2.
5. Killed his father and married his mother
6. The Chorus says that Teiresias is ___ in Ode I.
7. King of Corinth who raised the abandoned infant Oedipus
8. Oedipus ___ himself with the brooches from Iocaste's dress.
9. City being destroyed by a plague because of an unsolved murder
10. They will follow the killer wherever he goes.
11. Author of Oedipus Rex
12. Infant Oedipus had been left in the shadow of Mt. ___.
13. The Chorus prays to ___. Artemis, & Apollo for help.
14. A ___ spared infant Oedipus's life.
15. City in which Oedipus was raised
16. A ___ had warned Oedipus of his fate.

A=11	B=13	C=8	D=2
E=4	F=6	G=15	H=9
I=5	J=3	K=10	L=16
M=14	N=12	O=1	P=7

Oedipus Word Search 1

```
A K I T H A I R O N E E I S T S Q E F P
H N C O H P L D D B X X O H R A H P U L
U S T A E T R D E N O I C E A T F I R V
B O A I T D T O S L D L A P I Y A S I N
R P T S G H I F P Y O E S H T R N O E H
I H H N V O A P V H S Z T E O M T D S Q
S O E V J Y N R U D E R E R R E I E F K
K C N S Z X T E S S E C Q D B R S B L C
R L A C U V N S Q I S N Y Z X O T T A V
B E T L N I K N S T S D O G K P R H P Y
H S H C Y L C G L R L R E U D E O E O K
V K E F R I L I H A X A W L E C P B L W
K B S Z K E N J D G V Z I C P M H E L V
N K P R O L O G U E S T R O P H E S O Q
H R I W X V R N J D P M H R S X I N S T
Z G S K H G C K S Y H Q X I N H S N T G
R E L I E F F X K N I G B N S K W C R T
T E I R E S I A S S N M Z T B L I N D S
P O L Y B O S Y Z S X S C H O R A G O S
```

A ___ had warned Oedipus of his fate. (8)
A ___ spared infant Oedipus's life. (8)
Arrogance demonstrated by a character as a result of pride or passion (6)
Author of Oedipus Rex (9)
Blind prophet (9)
City being destroyed by a plague because of an unsolved murder (6)
City in which Oedipus was raised (7)
Destroyed herself after Oedipus correctly answered her riddle (6)
Father of Greek Theatre (7)
Feeling Oedipus has when he hears the King of Corinth is dead (6)
He is most concerned about Laios's murder. (6)
He took over as the King of Thebes. (5)
Infant Oedipus had been left in the shadow of Mt. ___. (9)
Introduces the main characters in the beginning of a play (8)
Iocaste commits this. (7)
Killed his father and married his mother (7)
King of Corinth who raised the abandoned infant Oedipus (7)
King of Thebes who was killed at a place where 3 roads meet (5)
Last song of the play, usually contains a moral lesson (6)
Leader of the chorus (8)
Location of Apollo's temple (6)
Movement of the chorus from left to right across the stage (11)
Movement of the chorus from right to left across the stage (7)
Oedipus ___ himself with the brooches from Iocaste's dress. (6)
Oedipus accused Creon of being a ___ at the opening of Scene 2 Ode 2. (7)
Oedipus follows his own edict and goes into self-___. (5)
One of Oedipus's daughters (8)
Play that comically portrayed mythological stories or poked fun at politics (5)
Purification of a character's emotions; an emotional release (9)
Queen of Corinth feared by Oedipus (6)
Resolution of the main conflict in a play (10)
Scene in a play (7)
Serious play in which the main character suffers from a flaw (7)
Songs that comment on the action of the play or its characters (4)
The Chorus prays to ___. Artemis, & Apollo for help. (6)
The Chorus says that Teiresias is ___ in Ode I. (5)
They will follow the killer wherever he goes. (6)
Wife of Laios and Oedipus (7)

Oedipus Word Search 1 Answer Key

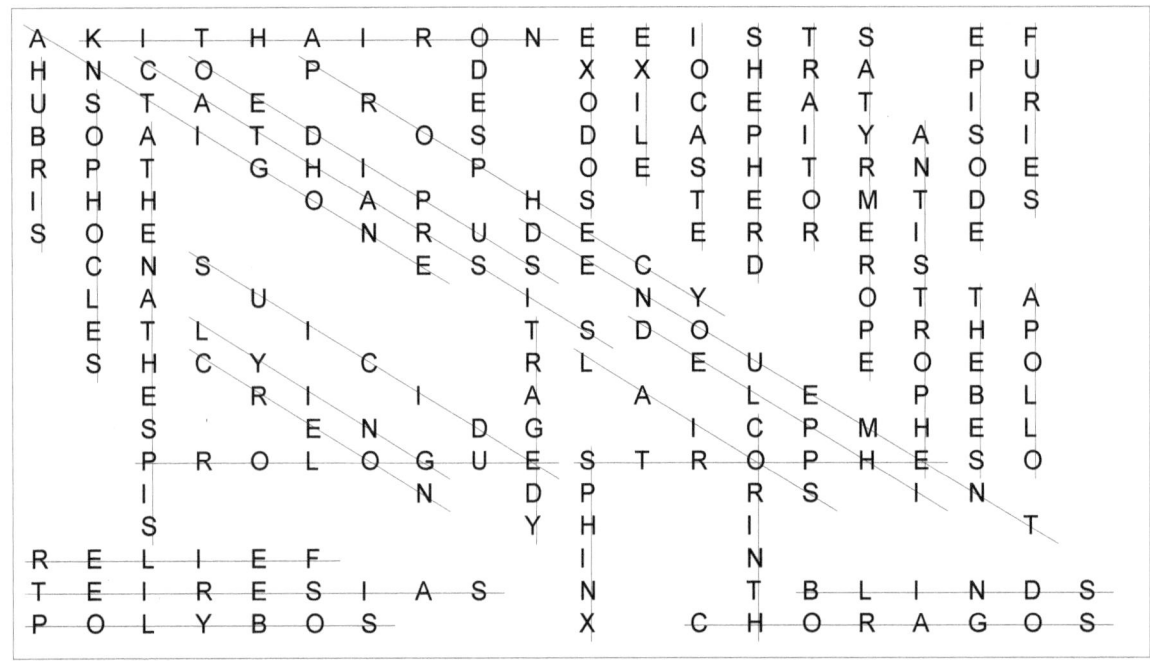

A ___ had warned Oedipus of his fate. (8)
A ___ spared infant Oedipus's life. (8)
Arrogance demonstrated by a character as a result of pride or passion (6)
Author of Oedipus Rex (9)
Blind prophet (9)
City being destroyed by a plague because of an unsolved murder (6)
City in which Oedipus was raised (7)
Destroyed herself after Oedipus correctly answered her riddle (6)
Father of Greek Theatre (7)
Feeling Oedipus has when he hears the King of Corinth is dead (6)
He is most concerned about Laios's murder. (6)
He took over as the King of Thebes. (5)
Infant Oedipus had been left in the shadow of Mt. ___. (9)
Introduces the main characters in the beginning of a play (8)
Iocaste commits this. (7)
Killed his father and married his mother (7)
King of Corinth who raised the abandoned infant Oedipus (7)
King of Thebes who was killed at a place where 3 roads meet (5)
Last song of the play, usually contains a moral lesson (6)
Leader of the chorus (8)

Location of Apollo's temple (6)
Movement of the chorus from left to right across the stage (11)
Movement of the chorus from right to left across the stage (7)
Oedipus ___ himself with the brooches from Iocaste's dress. (6)
Oedipus accused Creon of being a ___ at the opening of Scene 2 Ode 2. (7)
Oedipus follows his own edict and goes into self-___. (5)
One of Oedipus's daughters (8)
Play that comically portrayed mythological stories or poked fun at politics (5)
Purification of a character's emotions; an emotional release (9)
Queen of Corinth feared by Oedipus (6)
Resolution of the main conflict in a play (10)
Scene in a play (7)
Serious play in which the main character suffers from a flaw (7)
Songs that comment on the action of the play or its characters (4)
The Chorus prays to ___. Artemis, & Apollo for help. (6)
The Chorus says that Teiresias is ___ in Ode I. (5)
They will follow the killer wherever he goes. (6)
Wife of Laios and Oedipus (7)

Oedipus Word Search 2

```
C V V R M M H I V Q A P O L L O P K R Z
O W M V T G L W O M D Z R V J Q D Y Q F
R B X X G K M S T C P M W T B Z Y Z F R
I L J Q Y B K M M R A P S L K Y S M C H
N Z V N T X C M H F C S T P G D D G L T
T Z P W P M R Y C V T Z T Z W V B B S D
H H J N R X N Z X R S L W E Z P C Q O M
F D G T M K N Q P F J D C H P R V F P M
G R H K R S B Y N N R V W C Y O T V H N
J P L G T D F L M V H B P C F P T W O W
B C A G W H K N N D L V R D D H R H C S
Q T N F H C I P T B S P H W N E C X L X
J W T C X N T S F X B Q Y Y L C C F E B
C B I J R Q H V W E T D P O L Y B O S J
L S G C Y V A K J W X K B F Y L P H Z V
R T O J R S I L R L L I B M D W C B B C
J M N X P E R N Y A X B L T T B T C H C
T H E B E S O S U I C I D E B L I N D S
J T R S V H N N D O N W O I N J S G D D
R R E S R E L B B S V G E R K V F L E W
J A L W P P L Q M K Q M D E V R U M L M
S I I A T H E N A C H C I S M E R O P E
M T E H K E I B M R K K P I R B I B H Y
P O F Y N R V N J G K D U A M R E F I X
D R T M K D F J X X Z N S S W X S B D G
```

A ___ had warned Oedipus of his fate. (8)
A ___ spared infant Oedipus's life. (8)
Author of Oedipus Rex (9)
Blind prophet (9)
City being destroyed by a plague because of an unsolved murder (6)
City in which Oedipus was raised (7)
Destroyed herself after Oedipus correctly answered her riddle (6)
Feeling Oedipus has when he hears the King of Corinth is dead (6)
He is most concerned about Laios's murder. (6)
He took over as the King of Thebes. (5)
Infant Oedipus had been left in the shadow of Mt. ___. (9)
Iocaste commits this. (7)
Killed his father and married his mother (7)
King of Corinth who raised the abandoned infant Oedipus (7)
King of Thebes who was killed at a place where 3 roads meet (5)
Location of Apollo's temple (6)
Oedipus ___ himself with the brooches from Iocaste's dress. (6)
Oedipus accused Creon of being a ___ at the opening of Scene 2 Ode 2. (7)
Oedipus follows his own edict and goes into self-___. (5)
One of Oedipus's daughters (8)
Queen of Corinth feared by Oedipus (6)
The Chorus prays to ___. Artemis, & Apollo for help. (6)
The Chorus says that Teiresias is ___ in Ode I. (5)
They will follow the killer wherever he goes. (6)
Wife of Laios and Oedipus (7)

Oedipus Word Search 2 Answer Key

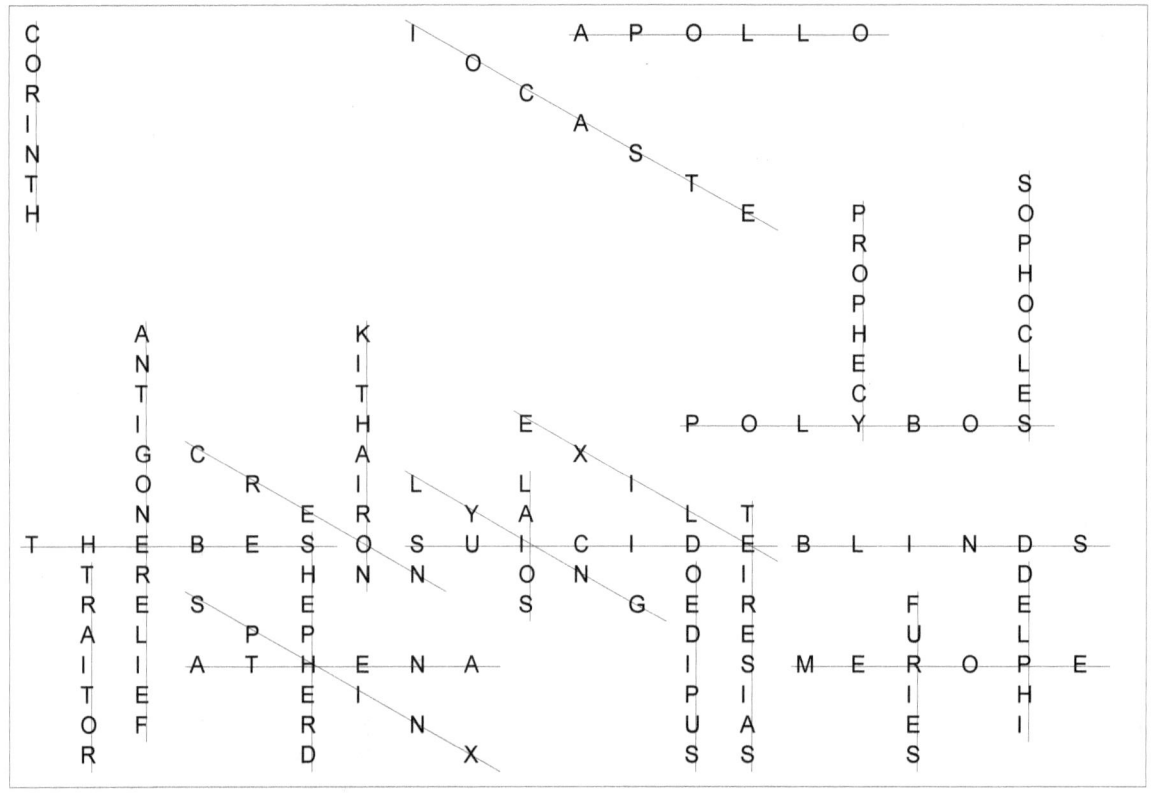

A ___ had warned Oedipus of his fate. (8)
A ___ spared infant Oedipus's life. (8)
Author of Oedipus Rex (9)
Blind prophet (9)
City being destroyed by a plague because of an unsolved murder (6)
City in which Oedipus was raised (7)
Destroyed herself after Oedipus correctly answered her riddle (6)
Feeling Oedipus has when he hears the King of Corinth is dead (6)
He is most concerned about Laios's murder. (6)
He took over as the King of Thebes. (5)
Infant Oedipus had been left in the shadow of Mt. ___. (9)
Iocaste commits this. (7)
Killed his father and married his mother (7)
King of Corinth who raised the abandoned infant Oedipus (7)
King of Thebes who was killed at a place where 3 roads meet (5)
Location of Apollo's temple (6)
Oedipus ___ himself with the brooches from Iocaste's dress. (6)
Oedipus accused Creon of being a ___ at the opening of Scene 2 Ode 2. (7)
Oedipus follows his own edict and goes into self-___. (5)
One of Oedipus's daughters (8)
Queen of Corinth feared by Oedipus (6)
The Chorus prays to ___. Artemis, & Apollo for help. (6)
The Chorus says that Teiresias is ___ in Ode I. (5)
They will follow the killer wherever he goes. (6)
Wife of Laios and Oedipus (7)

Oedipus Word Search 3

```
K I T H A I R O N M E X I L E T G S A N
N X Y F F N Q R V H T C O B K R F P N B
T P W T W S T K T D J Q C M K A W H T Z
C R S M T H Z I F E K G A S V I G I I W
S A T Y R E L Z G N M J S B P T G N S P
L K T R V P W P S O C V T T T O Z X T K
L H L H K H S R T U N X E N R R L B R G
F Y A S A E K P Q E V E W Z Z O S M O N
J F I H J R G M B M B X H G Z Q P D P G
L L O N Z D S X B E M J S Y L F M H H N
T R S X G D J I L N K B H N F L F Y E H
E Q P S B H P Y S T S O P H O C L E S Y
I T H E B E S R B B B T L X D D P L D G
R Q S F B F E W O R N Q V K P N O H Z R
E S G H P L U X Z L E C R K G A L U W S
S L K T C R I R O Z O L R T B T Y B O F
I P E G O T O N I D T G I E H B R D S
A R P H R Y R P D E O Y U E O E O I E B
S U I C I D E A H S S S D E F N S S V
Z J S G N Y C R G E V L E C J A T P R D
F S O G T B Y O B E C M L V C T C L I Y
W H D Z H N Y D W H D Y P M L F T H T S
S M E R O P E O F F C Y H A P O L L O X
C H O R A G O S S O E D I P U S Q V H C
```

ANTIGONE	CREON	IOCASTE	POLYBOS	STROPHE
ANTISTROPHE	DELPHI	KITHAIRON	PROLOGUE	SUICIDE
APOLLO	DENOUEMENT	LAIOS	PROPHECY	TEIRESIAS
ATHENA	EPISODE	LYING	RELIEF	THEBES
BLINDS	EXILE	MEROPE	SATYR	THESPIS
CATHARSIS	EXODOS	ODES	SHEPHERD	TRAGEDY
CHORAGOS	FURIES	OEDIPUS	SOPHOCLES	TRAITOR
CORINTH	HUBRIS	PARODOS	SPHINX	

Oedipus Word Search 3 Answer Key

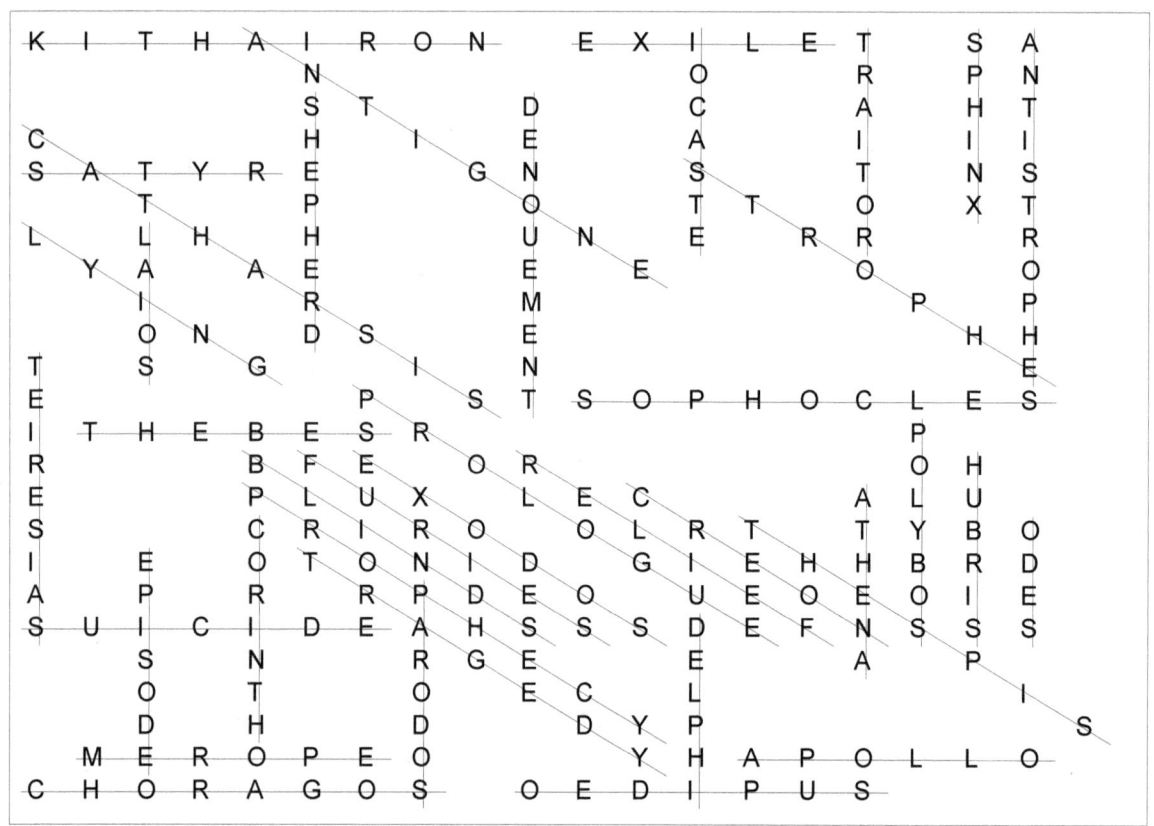

ANTIGONE	CREON	IOCASTE	POLYBOS	STROPHE
ANTISTROPHE	DELPHI	KITHAIRON	PROLOGUE	SUICIDE
APOLLO	DENOUEMENT	LAIOS	PROPHECY	TEIRESIAS
ATHENA	EPISODE	LYING	RELIEF	THEBES
BLINDS	EXILE	MEROPE	SATYR	THESPIS
CATHARSIS	EXODOS	ODES	SHEPHERD	TRAGEDY
CHORAGOS	FURIES	OEDIPUS	SOPHOCLES	TRAITOR
CORINTH	HUBRIS	PARODOS	SPHINX	

Oedipus Word Search 4

```
V L J S L W Y D N V C T K H S K X S M Z
T V Z O K C B P N Q R H Y V L D G H I T
K D Q P D L Z P M H P M T R F X P E O H
V P N H P H L L H X Z O M N V N S P C C
K W C O O V V A V W C E P W J H Q H A Z
J Y S C L N P I D D Y D X B P G L E S S
D M K L Y K Q O M G M I B N Q Z X R T C
Y T H E B E S S D J S P H I N X T D E M
R B L S O H M K M N K U Q Y R Z F C L V
X N L K S V H M I X P S I V E C T R Y T
W X Y I A F W E F T T S W C L M Z E I Y
A T H E N A P R O P H E C Y I C P O N H
H P N G T D Y O K L A A G F E D F N G L
T X X H I K S P V S P G I U F J E T T V
Q E N M G Z D E P P O P X R T R D R X V
W C I R O X E E X I L E V I O W T A X X
N O D R N L L H C F L P C E D N W I G Y
M R J Q E B P M Y S O N T S J R N T C N
L I G X K S H P M Y Q H C Q N W X O R V
P N Z C Z Q I T F P F T P X X P W R Q R
W T H X N S M A Y Q V G P B S M M X V Z
Y H H K Z C G W S W G Q M G W H P V B Q
M R L Q J N V L B M F X Q Q Q L K C B V
R V G Y D L J M M G N C N R J P G T C F
```

ANTIGONE	CREON	KITHAIRON	POLYBOS	SPHINX
APOLLO	DELPHI	LAIOS	PROPHECY	SUICIDE
ATHENA	EXILE	LYING	RELIEF	TEIRESIAS
BLINDS	FURIES	MEROPE	SHEPHERD	THEBES
CORINTH	IOCASTE	OEDIPUS	SOPHOCLES	TRAITOR

Oedipus Word Search 4 Answer Key

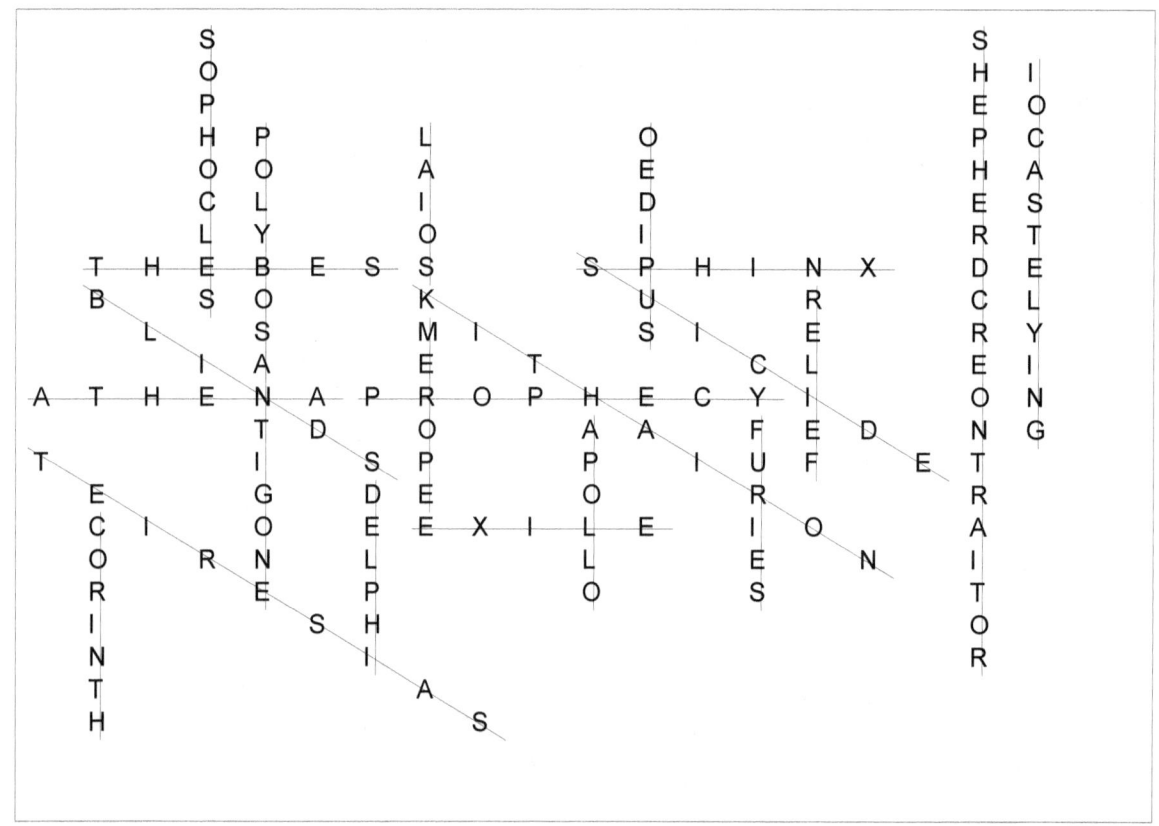

ANTIGONE	CREON	KITHAIRON	POLYBOS	SPHINX
APOLLO	DELPHI	LAIOS	PROPHECY	SUICIDE
ATHENA	EXILE	LYING	RELIEF	TEIRESIAS
BLINDS	FURIES	MEROPE	SHEPHERD	THEBES
CORINTH	IOCASTE	OEDIPUS	SOPHOCLES	TRAITOR

Oedipus Crossword 1

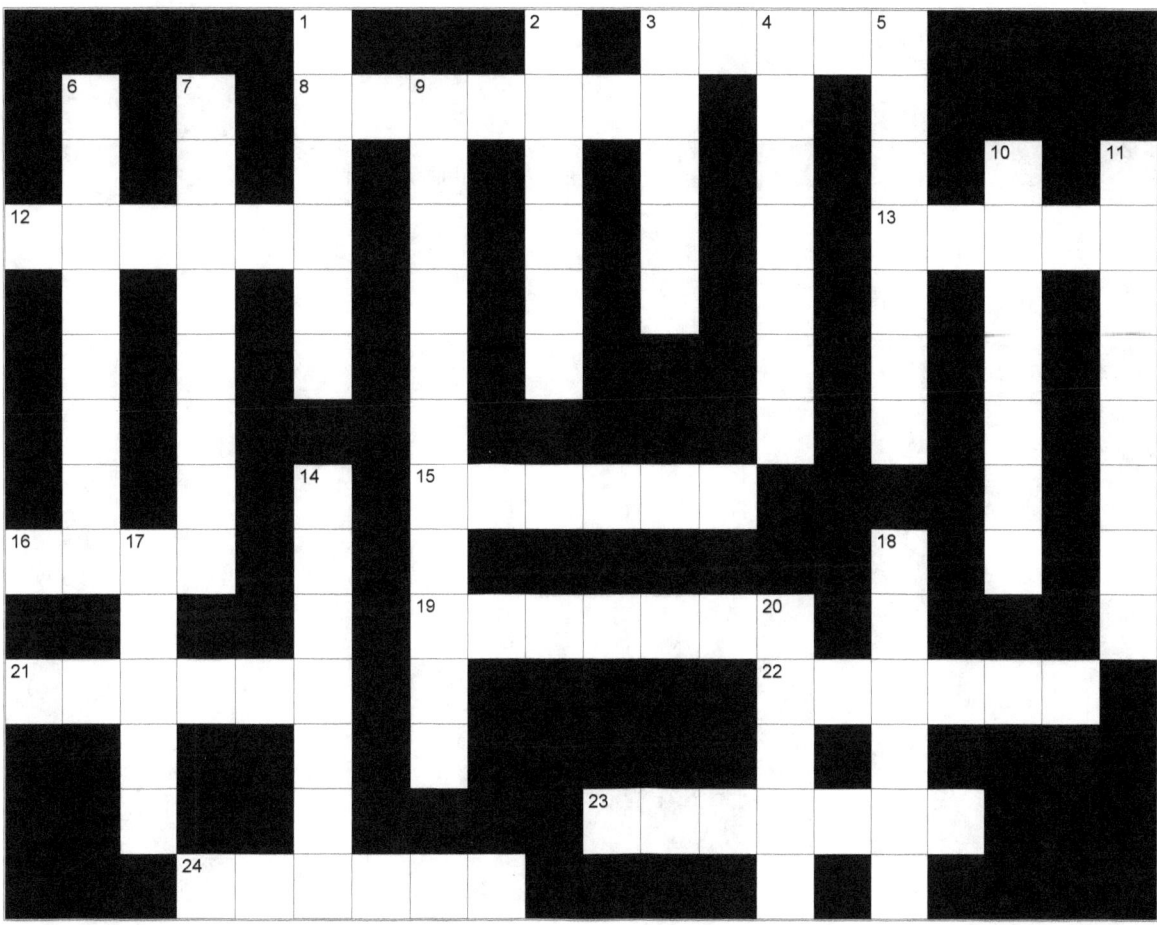

Across
3. King of Thebes who was killed at a place where 3 roads meet
8. Serious play in which the main character suffers from a flaw
12. Queen of Corinth feared by Oedipus
13. He took over as the King of Thebes.
15. Feeling Oedipus has when he hears the King of Corinth is dead
16. Songs that comment on the action of the play or its characters
19. Opening song as the chorus makes its entrance
21. Oedipus ___ himself with the brooches from Iocaste's dress.
22. He is most concerned about Laios's murder.
23. King of Corinth who raised the abandoned infant Oedipus
24. City being destroyed by a plague because of an unsolved murder

Down
1. The Chorus prays to ___. Artemis, & Apollo for help.
2. Location of Apollo's temple
3. The Chorus says that Teiresias is ___ in Ode I.
4. Wife of Laios and Oedipus
5. Iocaste commits this.
6. A ___ spared infant Oedipus's life.
7. Leader of the chorus
9. Movement of the chorus from left to right across the stage
10. Killed his father and married his mother
11. One of Oedipus's daughters
14. Scene in a play
17. Oedipus follows his own edict and goes into self-___.
18. Last song of the play, usually contains a moral lesson
20. Play that comically portrayed mythological stories or poked fun at politics

Oedipus Crossword 1 Answer Key

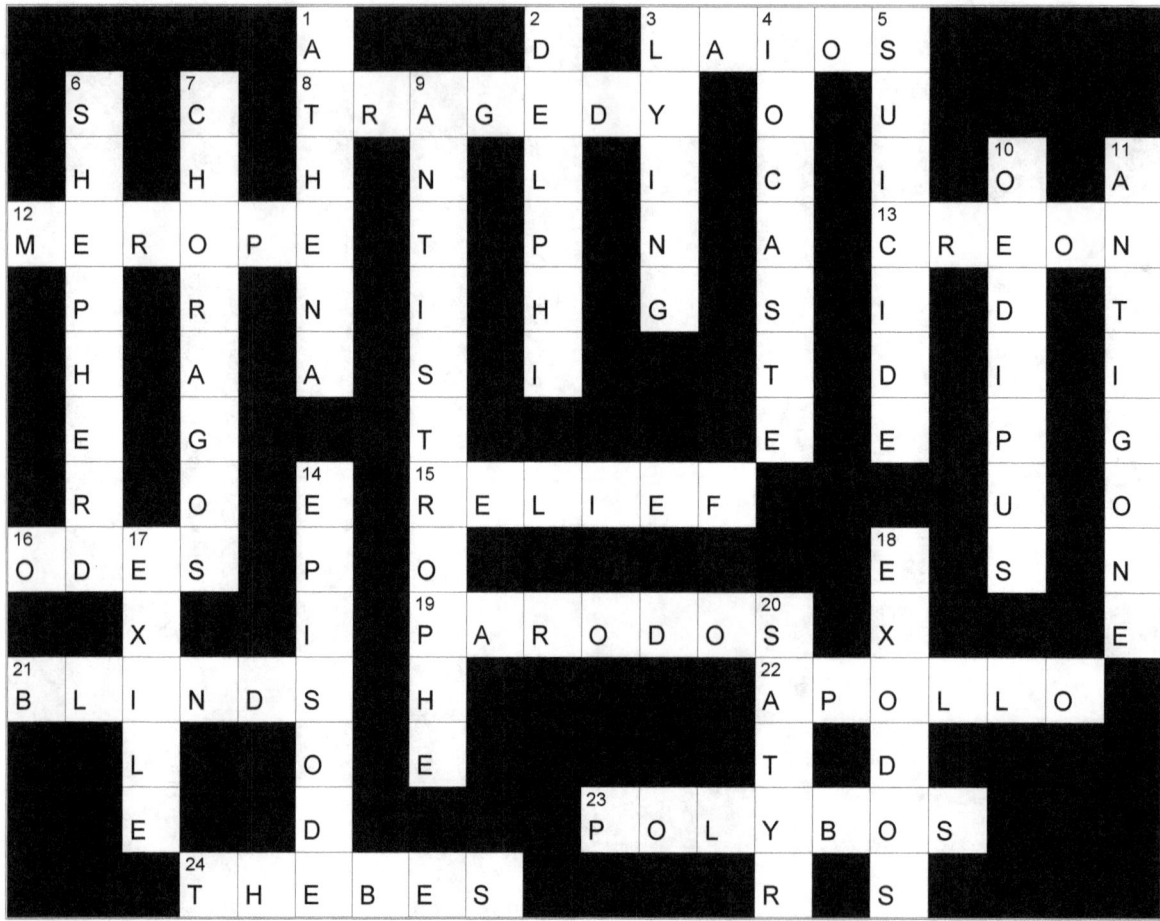

Across

3. King of Thebes who was killed at a place where 3 roads meet
8. Serious play in which the main character suffers from a flaw
12. Queen of Corinth feared by Oedipus
13. He took over as the King of Thebes.
15. Feeling Oedipus has when he hears the King of Corinth is dead
16. Songs that comment on the action of the play or its characters
19. Opening song as the chorus makes its entrance
21. Oedipus ___ himself with the brooches from Iocaste's dress.
22. He is most concerned about Laios's murder.
23. King of Corinth who raised the abandoned infant Oedipus
24. City being destroyed by a plague because of an unsolved murder

Down

1. The Chorus prays to ___. Artemis, & Apollo for help.
2. Location of Apollo's temple
3. The Chorus says that Teiresias is ___ in Ode I.
4. Wife of Laios and Oedipus
5. Iocaste commits this.
6. A ___ spared infant Oedipus's life.
7. Leader of the chorus
9. Movement of the chorus from left to right across the stage
10. Killed his father and married his mother
11. One of Oedipus's daughters
14. Scene in a play
17. Oedipus follows his own edict and goes into self-___.
18. Last song of the play, usually contains a moral lesson
20. Play that comically portrayed mythological stories or poked fun at politics

Oedipus Crossword 2

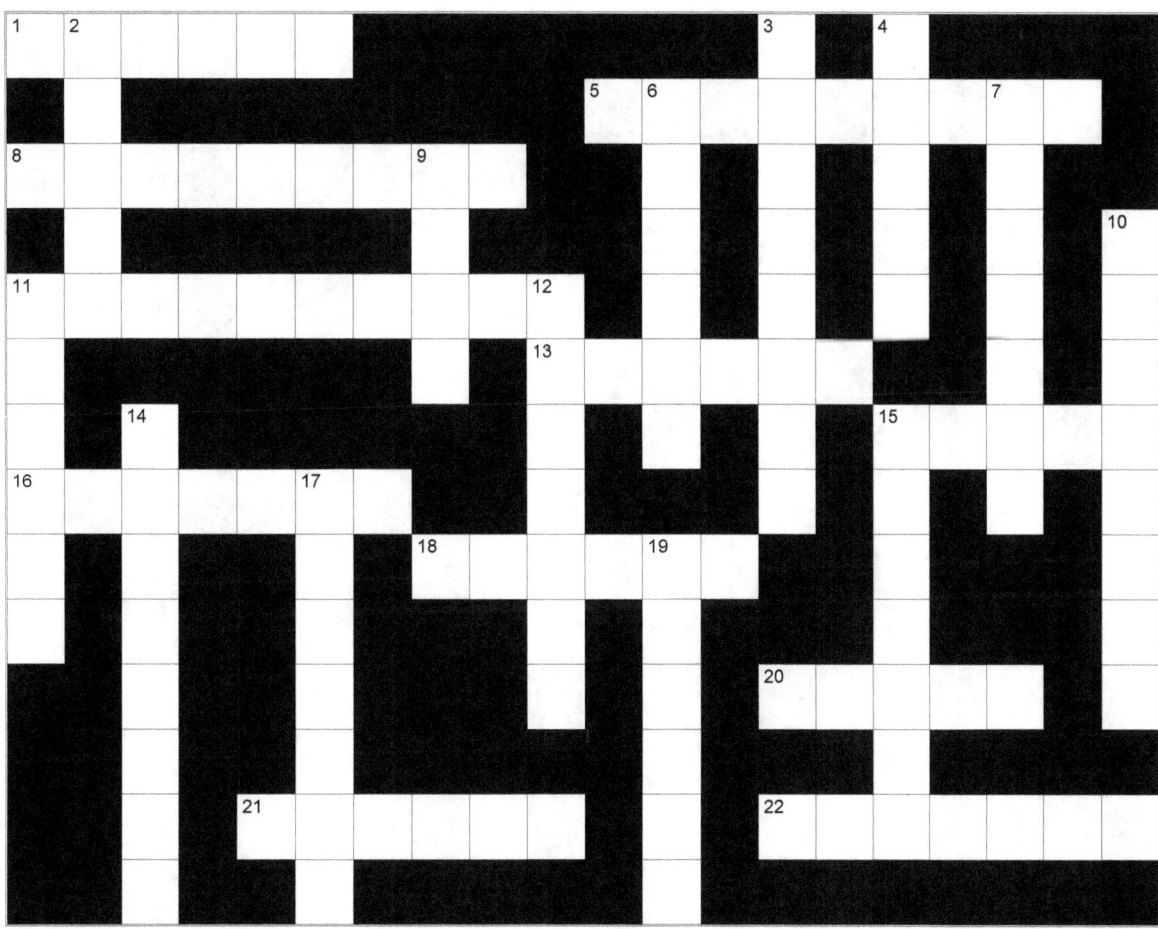

Across
1. Queen of Corinth feared by Oedipus
5. Purification of a character's emotions; an emotional release
8. Infant Oedipus had been left in the shadow of Mt. ___.
11. Resolution of the main conflict in a play
13. Feeling Oedipus has when he hears the King of Corinth is dead
15. Play that comically portrayed mythological stories or poked fun at politics
16. Opening song as the chorus makes its entrance
18. City being destroyed by a plague because of an unsolved murder
20. The Chorus says that Teiresias is ___ in Ode I.
21. They will follow the killer wherever he goes.
22. Father of Greek Theatre

Down
2. Oedipus follows his own edict and goes into self-___.
3. A ___ spared infant Oedipus's life.
4. He took over as the King of Thebes.
6. He is most concerned about Laios's murder.
7. Wife of Laios and Oedipus
9. Songs that comment on the action of the play or its characters
10. Leader of the chorus
11. Location of Apollo's temple
12. Serious play in which the main character suffers from a flaw
14. A ___ had warned Oedipus of his fate.
15. Iocaste commits this.
17. Killed his father and married his mother
19. Last song of the play, usually contains a moral lesson

Oedipus Crossword 2 Answer Key

Across
1. Queen of Corinth feared by Oedipus
5. Purification of a character's emotions; an emotional release
8. Infant Oedipus had been left in the shadow of Mt. ___.
11. Resolution of the main conflict in a play
13. Feeling Oedipus has when he hears the King of Corinth is dead
15. Play that comically portrayed mythological stories or poked fun at politics
16. Opening song as the chorus makes its entrance
18. City being destroyed by a plague because of an unsolved murder
20. The Chorus says that Teiresias is ___ in Ode I.
21. They will follow the killer wherever he goes.
22. Father of Greek Theatre

Down
2. Oedipus follows his own edict and goes into self-___.
3. A ___ spared infant Oedipus's life.
4. He took over as the King of Thebes.
6. He is most concerned about Laios's murder.
7. Wife of Laios and Oedipus
9. Songs that comment on the action of the play or its characters
10. Leader of the chorus
11. Location of Apollo's temple
12. Serious play in which the main character suffers from a flaw
14. A ___ had warned Oedipus of his fate.
15. Iocaste commits this.
17. Killed his father and married his mother
19. Last song of the play, usually contains a moral lesson

Oedipus Crossword 3

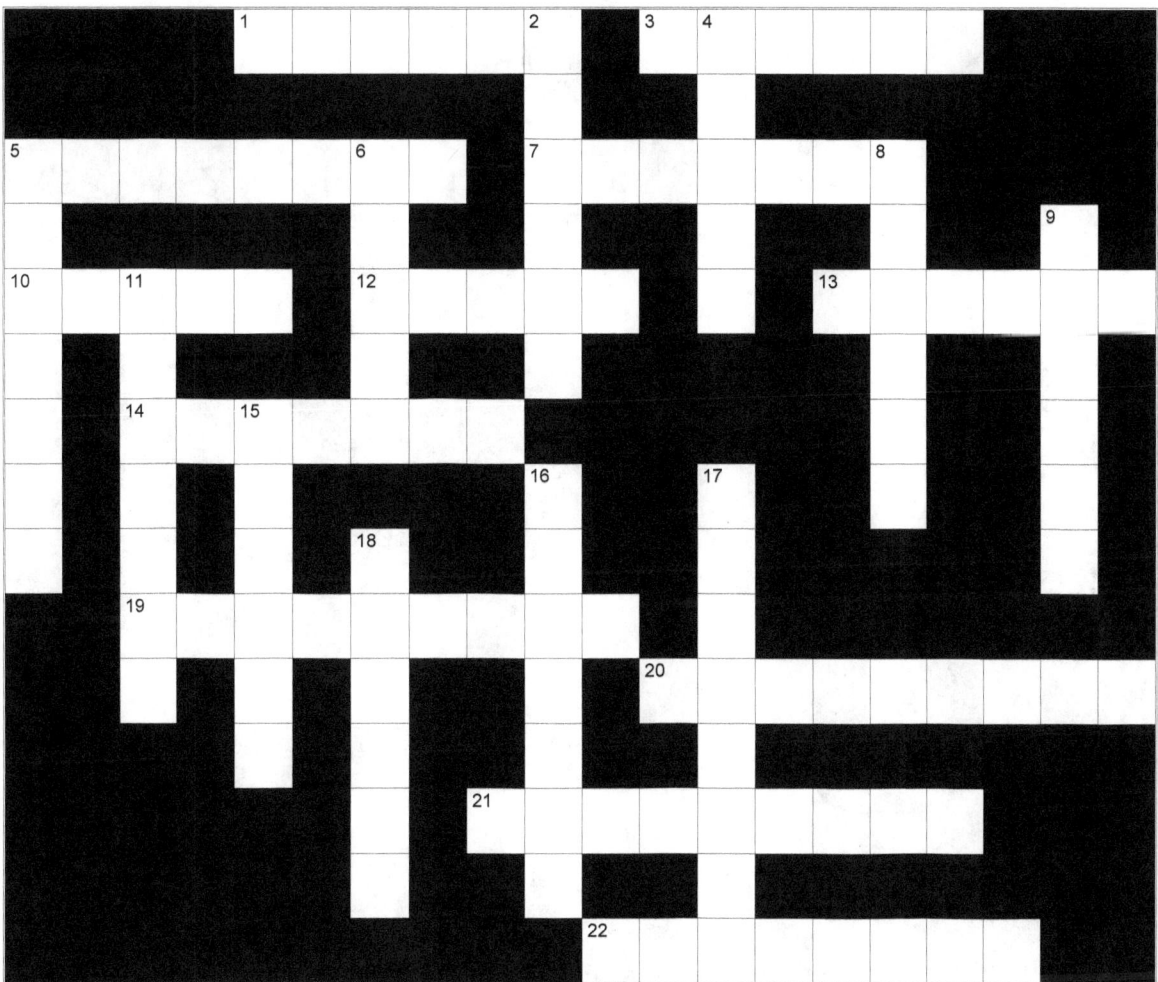

Across
1. The Chorus prays to ___. Artemis, & Apollo for help.
3. Oedipus ___ himself with the brooches from Iocaste's dress.
5. A ___ had warned Oedipus of his fate.
7. Killed his father and married his mother
10. King of Thebes who was killed at a place where 3 roads meet
12. Oedipus follows his own edict and goes into self-___.
13. City being destroyed by a plague because of an unsolved murder
14. City in which Oedipus was raised
19. Blind prophet
20. Infant Oedipus had been left in the shadow of Mt. ___.
21. Author of Oedipus Rex
22. A ___ spared infant Oedipus's life.

Down
2. He is most concerned about Laios's murder.
4. The Chorus says that Teiresias is ___ in Ode I.
5. King of Corinth who raised the abandoned infant Oedipus
6. He took over as the King of Thebes.
8. Destroyed herself after Oedipus correctly answered her riddle
9. Queen of Corinth feared by Oedipus
11. Wife of Laios and Oedipus
15. Feeling Oedipus has when he hears the King of Corinth is dead
16. Oedipus accused Creon of being a ___ at the opening of Scene 2 Ode 2.
17. One of Oedipus's daughters
18. Location of Apollo's temple

Oedipus Crossword 3 Answer Key

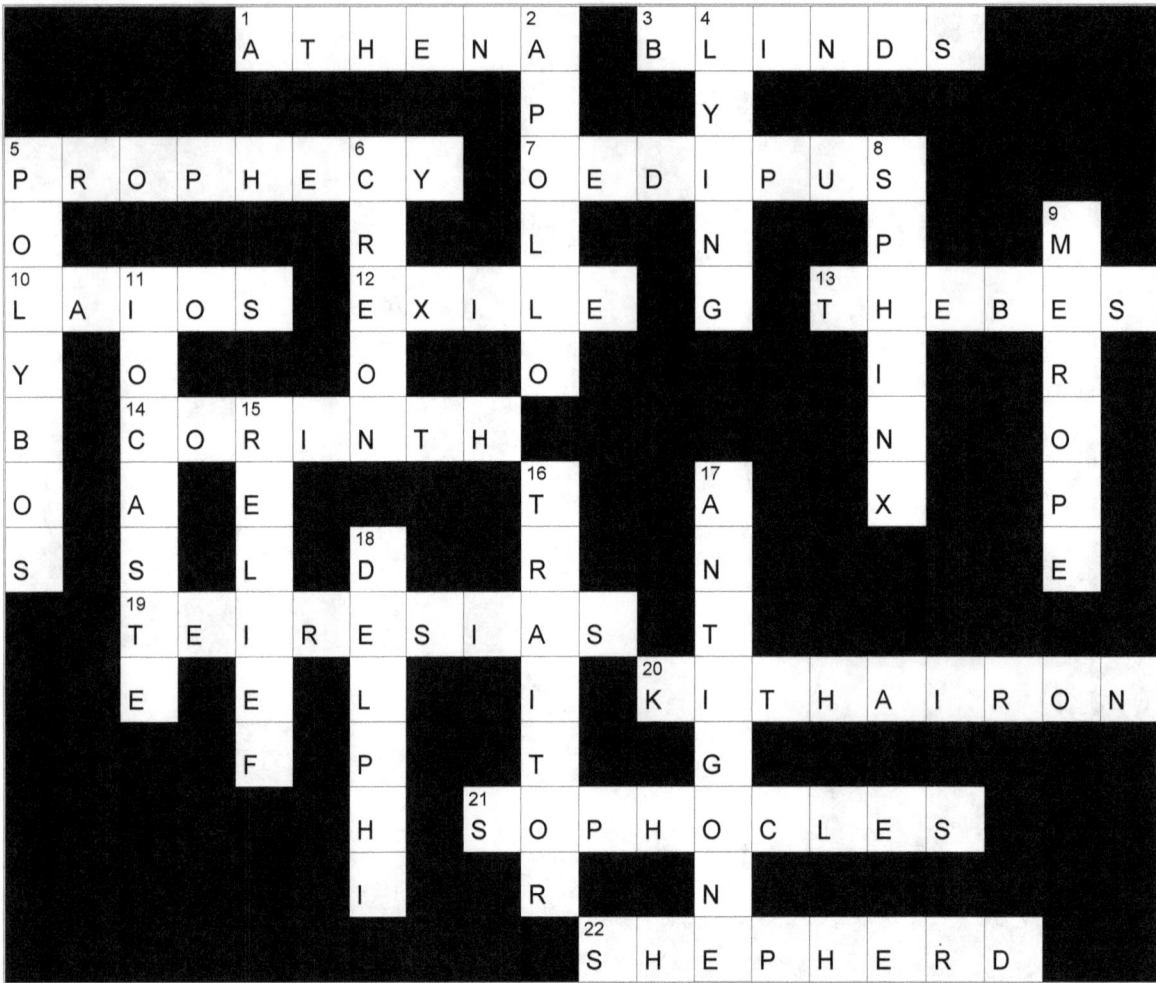

Across
1. The Chorus prays to ___. Artemis, & Apollo for help.
3. Oedipus ___ himself with the brooches from Iocaste's dress.
5. A ___ had warned Oedipus of his fate.
7. Killed his father and married his mother
10. King of Thebes who was killed at a place where 3 roads meet
12. Oedipus follows his own edict and goes into self-___.
13. City being destroyed by a plague because of an unsolved murder
14. City in which Oedipus was raised
19. Blind prophet
20. Infant Oedipus had been left in the shadow of Mt. ___.
21. Author of Oedipus Rex
22. A ___ spared infant Oedipus's life.

Down
2. He is most concerned about Laios's murder.
4. The Chorus says that Teiresias is ___ in Ode I.
5. King of Corinth who raised the abandoned infant Oedipus
6. He took over as the King of Thebes.
8. Destroyed herself after Oedipus correctly answered her riddle
9. Queen of Corinth feared by Oedipus
11. Wife of Laios and Oedipus
15. Feeling Oedipus has when he hears the King of Corinth is dead
16. Oedipus accused Creon of being a ___ at the opening of Scene 2 Ode 2.
17. One of Oedipus's daughters
18. Location of Apollo's temple

Oedipus Crossword 4

Across
1. They will follow the killer wherever he goes.
3. Oedipus accused Creon of being a ___ at the opening of Scene 2 Ode 2.
5. Infant Oedipus had been left in the shadow of Mt. ___.
9. A ___ spared infant Oedipus's life.
12. One of Oedipus's daughters
13. King of Thebes who was killed at a place where 3 roads meet
14. Oedipus ___ himself with the brooches from Iocaste's dress.
18. City being destroyed by a plague because of an unsolved murder
19. Feeling Oedipus has when he hears the King of Corinth is dead
20. City in which Oedipus was raised
21. Killed his father and married his mother

Down
2. Oedipus follows his own edict and goes into self-___.
4. The Chorus prays to ___, Artemis, & Apollo for help.
6. Wife of Laios and Oedipus
7. The Chorus says that Teiresias is ___ in Ode I.
8. He is most concerned about Laios's murder.
9. Iocaste commits this.
10. King of Corinth who raised the abandoned infant Oedipus
11. Blind prophet
15. Location of Apollo's temple
16. Queen of Corinth feared by Oedipus
17. Destroyed herself after Oedipus correctly answered her riddle

Oedipus Crossword 4 Answer Key

Across
1. They will follow the killer wherever he goes.
3. Oedipus accused Creon of being a ___ at the opening of Scene 2 Ode 2.
5. Infant Oedipus had been left in the shadow of Mt. ___.
9. A ___ spared infant Oedipus's life.
12. One of Oedipus's daughters
13. King of Thebes who was killed at a place where 3 roads meet
14. Oedipus ___ himself with the brooches from Iocaste's dress.
18. City being destroyed by a plague because of an unsolved murder
19. Feeling Oedipus has when he hears the King of Corinth is dead
20. City in which Oedipus was raised
21. Killed his father and married his mother

Down
2. Oedipus follows his own edict and goes into self-___.
4. The Chorus prays to ___. Artemis, & Apollo for help.
6. Wife of Laios and Oedipus
7. The Chorus says that Teiresias is ___ in Ode I.
8. He is most concerned about Laios's murder.
9. Iocaste commits this.
10. King of Corinth who raised the abandoned infant Oedipus
11. Blind prophet
15. Location of Apollo's temple
16. Queen of Corinth feared by Oedipus
17. Destroyed herself after Oedipus correctly answered her riddle

Oedipus

PROLOGUE	CREON	IOCASTE	HUBRIS	CHORAGOS
ANTIGONE	APOLLO	PARODOS	TEIRESIAS	EXILE
THEBES	SUICIDE	FREE SPACE	FURIES	BLINDS
CORINTH	EPISODE	LAIOS	POLYBOS	SATYR
DELPHI	DENOUEMENT	ATHENA	TRAGEDY	PROPHECY

Oedipus

MEROPE	KITHAIRON	ODES	TRAITOR	SPHINX
EXODOS	STROPHE	LYING	CATHARSIS	OEDIPUS
SHEPHERD	SOPHOCLES	FREE SPACE	ANTISTROPHE	PROPHECY
TRAGEDY	ATHENA	DENOUEMENT	DELPHI	SATYR
POLYBOS	LAIOS	EPISODE	CORINTH	BLINDS

Oedipus

CREON	APOLLO	SPHINX	THESPIS	STROPHE
DELPHI	ANTISTROPHE	SATYR	FURIES	ATHENA
KITHAIRON	IOCASTE	FREE SPACE	HUBRIS	CORINTH
ANTIGONE	PARODOS	TRAITOR	LAIOS	PROLOGUE
LYING	CHORAGOS	BLINDS	EPISODE	PROPHECY

Oedipus

DENOUEMENT	TRAGEDY	RELIEF	TEIRESIAS	THEBES
CATHARSIS	OEDIPUS	POLYBOS	SHEPHERD	SOPHOCLES
SUICIDE	EXILE	FREE SPACE	MEROPE	PROPHECY
EPISODE	BLINDS	CHORAGOS	LYING	PROLOGUE
LAIOS	TRAITOR	PARODOS	ANTIGONE	CORINTH

Oedipus

CORINTH	PARODOS	ANTIGONE	STROPHE	CREON
THEBES	OEDIPUS	SUICIDE	EXODOS	CHORAGOS
KITHAIRON	ATHENA	FREE SPACE	HUBRIS	ODES
BLINDS	TRAITOR	TEIRESIAS	FURIES	SHEPHERD
LAIOS	SOPHOCLES	RELIEF	IOCASTE	CATHARSIS

Oedipus

DELPHI	TRAGEDY	SATYR	LYING	PROPHECY
APOLLO	THESPIS	SPHINX	MEROPE	EXILE
POLYBOS	PROLOGUE	FREE SPACE	EPISODE	CATHARSIS
IOCASTE	RELIEF	SOPHOCLES	LAIOS	SHEPHERD
FURIES	TEIRESIAS	TRAITOR	BLINDS	ODES

Oedipus

APOLLO	IOCASTE	DENOUEMENT	ANTISTROPHE	TEIRESIAS
POLYBOS	MEROPE	ANTIGONE	TRAGEDY	SPHINX
SATYR	LAIOS	FREE SPACE	THEBES	ATHENA
CATHARSIS	CREON	CHORAGOS	OEDIPUS	BLINDS
RELIEF	PARODOS	PROPHECY	SUICIDE	FURIES

Oedipus

KITHAIRON	CORINTH	STROPHE	THESPIS	HUBRIS
ODES	SOPHOCLES	SHEPHERD	EXILE	LYING
DELPHI	EXODOS	FREE SPACE	PROLOGUE	FURIES
SUICIDE	PROPHECY	PARODOS	RELIEF	BLINDS
OEDIPUS	CHORAGOS	CREON	CATHARSIS	ATHENA

Oedipus

KITHAIRON	ATHENA	CHORAGOS	POLYBOS	SATYR
RELIEF	SPHINX	DELPHI	PARODOS	CATHARSIS
APOLLO	HUBRIS	FREE SPACE	SHEPHERD	DENOUEMENT
CREON	EXILE	OEDIPUS	THESPIS	ANTISTROPHE
TRAITOR	CORINTH	PROPHECY	THEBES	LYING

Oedipus

TEIRESIAS	EXODOS	BLINDS	LAIOS	ODES
SOPHOCLES	SUICIDE	MEROPE	ANTIGONE	IOCASTE
STROPHE	TRAGEDY	FREE SPACE	PROLOGUE	LYING
THEBES	PROPHECY	CORINTH	TRAITOR	ANTISTROPHE
THESPIS	OEDIPUS	EXILE	CREON	DENOUEMENT

Oedipus

SATYR	LYING	STROPHE	APOLLO	PROLOGUE
MEROPE	CORINTH	IOCASTE	ODES	LAIOS
KITHAIRON	EXILE	FREE SPACE	CATHARSIS	SHEPHERD
TEIRESIAS	OEDIPUS	THESPIS	SOPHOCLES	BLINDS
EXODOS	SPHINX	POLYBOS	CHORAGOS	ANTISTROPHE

Oedipus

THEBES	HUBRIS	ATHENA	RELIEF	CREON
TRAGEDY	PARODOS	PROPHECY	SUICIDE	ANTIGONE
TRAITOR	DELPHI	FREE SPACE	DENOUEMENT	ANTISTROPHE
CHORAGOS	POLYBOS	SPHINX	EXODOS	BLINDS
SOPHOCLES	THESPIS	OEDIPUS	TEIRESIAS	SHEPHERD

Oedipus

SUICIDE	CORINTH	DELPHI	DENOUEMENT	APOLLO
BLINDS	HUBRIS	PROPHECY	TRAITOR	RELIEF
ODES	SHEPHERD	FREE SPACE	KITHAIRON	PROLOGUE
CHORAGOS	STROPHE	EXODOS	EPISODE	ANTIGONE
MEROPE	THEBES	SOPHOCLES	OEDIPUS	IOCASTE

Oedipus

SPHINX	EXILE	THESPIS	TEIRESIAS	ANTISTROPHE
PARODOS	LAIOS	SATYR	TRAGEDY	LYING
CREON	FURIES	FREE SPACE	CATHARSIS	IOCASTE
OEDIPUS	SOPHOCLES	THEBES	MEROPE	ANTIGONE
EPISODE	EXODOS	STROPHE	CHORAGOS	PROLOGUE

Oedipus

SPHINX	CORINTH	BLINDS	RELIEF	STROPHE
TRAITOR	SATYR	TEIRESIAS	POLYBOS	EXODOS
EXILE	LYING	FREE SPACE	ANTIGONE	SUICIDE
ODES	DENOUEMENT	KITHAIRON	EPISODE	CATHARSIS
SHEPHERD	CHORAGOS	TRAGEDY	OEDIPUS	PROPHECY

Oedipus

FURIES	DELPHI	ATHENA	IOCASTE	LAIOS
MEROPE	SOPHOCLES	APOLLO	PROLOGUE	CREON
ANTISTROPHE	PARODOS	FREE SPACE	THESPIS	PROPHECY
OEDIPUS	TRAGEDY	CHORAGOS	SHEPHERD	CATHARSIS
EPISODE	KITHAIRON	DENOUEMENT	ODES	SUICIDE

Oedipus

ODES	DELPHI	TRAGEDY	ANTISTROPHE	STROPHE
THEBES	KITHAIRON	TEIRESIAS	EPISODE	FURIES
SATYR	HUBRIS	FREE SPACE	ATHENA	CATHARSIS
OEDIPUS	SPHINX	CHORAGOS	RELIEF	APOLLO
POLYBOS	CREON	CORINTH	EXODOS	SHEPHERD

Oedipus

SOPHOCLES	BLINDS	SUICIDE	ANTIGONE	LAIOS
EXILE	TRAITOR	MEROPE	PROLOGUE	THESPIS
IOCASTE	LYING	FREE SPACE	PARODOS	SHEPHERD
EXODOS	CORINTH	CREON	POLYBOS	APOLLO
RELIEF	CHORAGOS	SPHINX	OEDIPUS	CATHARSIS

Oedipus

BLINDS	HUBRIS	EXODOS	ANTIGONE	CATHARSIS
SHEPHERD	MEROPE	CREON	KITHAIRON	DENOUEMENT
OEDIPUS	SOPHOCLES	FREE SPACE	CHORAGOS	DELPHI
SPHINX	SUICIDE	EPISODE	PROPHECY	APOLLO
LAIOS	SATYR	TRAITOR	PARODOS	ATHENA

Oedipus

ANTISTROPHE	IOCASTE	FURIES	TRAGEDY	POLYBOS
THEBES	STROPHE	LYING	ODES	THESPIS
TEIRESIAS	EXILE	FREE SPACE	RELIEF	ATHENA
PARODOS	TRAITOR	SATYR	LAIOS	APOLLO
PROPHECY	EPISODE	SUICIDE	SPHINX	DELPHI

54
Copyrighted

Oedipus

EPISODE	STROPHE	APOLLO	OEDIPUS	CATHARSIS
DELPHI	PARODOS	TEIRESIAS	PROLOGUE	KITHAIRON
POLYBOS	SHEPHERD	FREE SPACE	THEBES	SATYR
IOCASTE	BLINDS	CORINTH	CREON	DENOUEMENT
MEROPE	SPHINX	ATHENA	RELIEF	PROPHECY

Oedipus

TRAGEDY	CHORAGOS	ANTIGONE	ODES	ANTISTROPHE
SUICIDE	LAIOS	EXODOS	EXILE	TRAITOR
SOPHOCLES	LYING	FREE SPACE	HUBRIS	PROPHECY
RELIEF	ATHENA	SPHINX	MEROPE	DENOUEMENT
CREON	CORINTH	BLINDS	IOCASTE	SATYR

Oedipus

SOPHOCLES	SUICIDE	ATHENA	TEIRESIAS	DELPHI
KITHAIRON	RELIEF	IOCASTE	PARODOS	THEBES
MEROPE	EPISODE	FREE SPACE	CHORAGOS	PROPHECY
SPHINX	LYING	TRAITOR	OEDIPUS	APOLLO
BLINDS	DENOUEMENT	PROLOGUE	STROPHE	FURIES

Oedipus

ANTISTROPHE	TRAGEDY	LAIOS	SATYR	CORINTH
CATHARSIS	ANTIGONE	SHEPHERD	EXODOS	HUBRIS
EXILE	THESPIS	FREE SPACE	POLYBOS	FURIES
STROPHE	PROLOGUE	DENOUEMENT	BLINDS	APOLLO
OEDIPUS	TRAITOR	LYING	SPHINX	PROPHECY

Oedipus

THEBES	HUBRIS	TRAGEDY	THESPIS	TRAITOR
ANTISTROPHE	LYING	CATHARSIS	ODES	POLYBOS
PROPHECY	ANTIGONE	FREE SPACE	SUICIDE	PROLOGUE
DENOUEMENT	BLINDS	EXILE	PARODOS	SHEPHERD
EPISODE	KITHAIRON	ATHENA	CORINTH	CHORAGOS

Oedipus

RELIEF	SOPHOCLES	SATYR	EXODOS	TEIRESIAS
IOCASTE	DELPHI	LAIOS	APOLLO	OEDIPUS
SPHINX	STROPHE	FREE SPACE	FURIES	CHORAGOS
CORINTH	ATHENA	KITHAIRON	EPISODE	SHEPHERD
PARODOS	EXILE	BLINDS	DENOUEMENT	PROLOGUE

Oedipus

THEBES	LYING	SPHINX	TEIRESIAS	EXILE
CATHARSIS	CHORAGOS	EXODOS	POLYBOS	PARODOS
ODES	CORINTH	FREE SPACE	FURIES	MEROPE
RELIEF	TRAGEDY	PROPHECY	PROLOGUE	LAIOS
EPISODE	DELPHI	ATHENA	DENOUEMENT	APOLLO

Oedipus

BLINDS	THESPIS	KITHAIRON	TRAITOR	STROPHE
SHEPHERD	IOCASTE	SUICIDE	HUBRIS	SATYR
SOPHOCLES	CREON	FREE SPACE	ANTISTROPHE	APOLLO
DENOUEMENT	ATHENA	DELPHI	EPISODE	LAIOS
PROLOGUE	PROPHECY	TRAGEDY	RELIEF	MEROPE

Oedipus

SPHINX	DENOUEMENT	POLYBOS	BLINDS	SHEPHERD
IOCASTE	TRAITOR	RELIEF	THEBES	CHORAGOS
ANTIGONE	EXILE	FREE SPACE	ATHENA	CORINTH
THESPIS	EXODOS	CATHARSIS	PROLOGUE	DELPHI
ODES	APOLLO	SOPHOCLES	FURIES	EPISODE

Oedipus

CREON	SUICIDE	PARODOS	TRAGEDY	MEROPE
PROPHECY	LYING	LAIOS	OEDIPUS	KITHAIRON
STROPHE	SATYR	FREE SPACE	ANTISTROPHE	EPISODE
FURIES	SOPHOCLES	APOLLO	ODES	DELPHI
PROLOGUE	CATHARSIS	EXODOS	THESPIS	CORINTH

Oedipus

MEROPE	SOPHOCLES	FURIES	DELPHI	LYING
EXODOS	RELIEF	CORINTH	EPISODE	THESPIS
STROPHE	CATHARSIS	FREE SPACE	APOLLO	LAIOS
TRAITOR	SPHINX	KITHAIRON	TEIRESIAS	IOCASTE
POLYBOS	SATYR	SUICIDE	CHORAGOS	ANTISTROPHE

Oedipus

CREON	SHEPHERD	EXILE	ATHENA	THEBES
HUBRIS	OEDIPUS	TRAGEDY	BLINDS	DENOUEMENT
PARODOS	PROPHECY	FREE SPACE	ANTIGONE	ANTISTROPHE
CHORAGOS	SUICIDE	SATYR	POLYBOS	IOCASTE
TEIRESIAS	KITHAIRON	SPHINX	TRAITOR	LAIOS

Oedipus Vocabulary Word List

No.	Word	Clue/Definition
1.	ABOMINATION	Anything greatly disliked or abhorred
2.	AUGURY	An event indicating important things to come: fortune telling
3.	BANE	A person or thing that ruins or spoils
4.	BASENESS	Characteristic of or befitting an inferior person or thing
5.	BATTENS	To thrive and prosper, especially at another's expense
6.	BEGETTING	Fathering; siring
7.	BESIEGER	An enemy who lays siege to your positions
8.	BRAZEN	Boldly shameless or impudent
9.	BROOCHES	Relatively large decorative pins or clasps
10.	COMPUNCTION	Any uneasiness or hesitation about the rightness of an action
11.	CONTAGION	The means by which a contagious disease is transmitted
12.	DECREPIT	Weakened by old age; feeble
13.	DEFILEMENT	To make foul, dirty, or unclean; pollute
14.	DIN	A loud, disturbing noise
15.	EASE	Freedom from difficulty or great effort
16.	EDICT	Any authoritative proclamation or command
17.	ENQUIRY	A seeking or request for truth, information, or knowledge
18.	EXECRABLE	Utterly detestable; abominable; very bad
19.	EXPELLED	Forced or drove out
20.	FACTION	A group or clique within a larger group, party, or government
21.	FRAILTY	Moral weakness; liability to yield to temptation
22.	GROUNDLESS	Without rational basis
23.	HARROWED	To break up soil with a toll consisting of a heavy frame with sharp teeth
24.	HEARTH	The floor of a fireplace, usually of stone or brick
25.	HELMSMAN	A person who steers a ship
26.	INSOLENCE	Rude or impertinent behavior or speech
27.	ISTHMUS	A narrow strip of land, bordered on both sides by water, connecting two larger bodies of land
28.	LIBERATOR	Someone who releases people from captivity or bondage
29.	LUSTRATION	The act of purifying by means of ceremony
30.	MALEDICTION	The utterance of a curse
31.	MAUNDERING	Moving or acting in an aimless or vague manner
32.	MUMMERY	Any performance or ceremony regarded as absurd or false
33.	NYMPHS	Female spirits who lived in forests, bodies of water, and other places outdoors
34.	OUTCAST	One who is rejected or discarded
35.	OVERWROUGHT	Extremely or excessively excited or agitated
36.	PARRICIDE	A person who kills his own parent
37.	PARRY	To turn aside; evade or dodge
38.	PASTURAGE	The activity or business of pasturing livestock
39.	PERQUISITES	Those things claimed as exclusive rights
40.	PESTILENCE	Something that is considered harmful, destructive, or evil
41.	PRESUME	To take for granted, assume, or suppose
42.	PRIMAL	Being first in time; original
43.	PRUDENT	Wise or judicious in practical affairs
44.	RANKLED	Caused keen irritation or bitter resentment
45.	REASSURED	Restored confidence to
46.	REGICIDE	The killing of a king
47.	RENOWN	Widespread and high repute; fame
48.	SCANT	To treat slightly or inadequately

Oedipus Vocabulary Word List Continued

No.	Word	Clue/Definition
49.	SEPULCHRE	A tomb, grave, or burial place
50.	SHROUD	A cloth or sheet in which a corpse is wrapped for burial
51.	SIRING	A father's children
52.	SOLEMN	Causing serious thoughts or a grave mood
53.	SOOTHSAYER	Person who professes to foretell events, fortune-teller
54.	SPLENDOR	Brilliant or gorgeous appearance
55.	SUPPLIANT	One who asks humbly and earnestly
56.	SUPPLICATION	To ask for humbly or earnestly, as by praying
57.	VENERATE	To regard or treat with reverence or respect
58.	VIGIL	A period of watchful attention maintained at night
59.	VOID	An empty space; emptiness
60.	WRETCHED	Very unfortunate in condition or circumstances

Oedipus Vocabulary Fill In The Blanks 1

1. One who asks humbly and earnestly
2. Moving or acting in an aimless or vague manner
3. Boldly shameless or impudent
4. A tomb, grave, or burial place
5. A group or clique within a larger group, party, or government
6. The act of purifying by means of ceremony
7. To thrive and prosper, especially at another's expense
8. Utterly detestable; abominable; very bad
9. Weakened by old age; feeble
10. Any uneasiness or hesitation about the rightness of an action
11. Something that is considered harmful, destructive, or evil
12. Extremely or excessively excited or agitated
13. The floor of a fireplace, usually of stone or brick
14. A loud, disturbing noise
15. An empty space; emptiness
16. Moral weakness; liability to yield to temptation
17. Restored confidence to
18. A person who kills his own parent
19. Person who professes to foretell events, fortune-teller
20. Freedom from difficulty or great effort

Oedipus Vocabulary Fill In The Blanks 1 Answer Key

SUPPLIANT	1. One who asks humbly and earnestly
MAUNDERING	2. Moving or acting in an aimless or vague manner
BRAZEN	3. Boldly shameless or impudent
SEPULCHRE	4. A tomb, grave, or burial place
FACTION	5. A group or clique within a larger group, party, or government
LUSTRATION	6. The act of purifying by means of ceremony
BATTENS	7. To thrive and prosper, especially at another's expense
EXECRABLE	8. Utterly detestable; abominable; very bad
DECREPIT	9. Weakened by old age; feeble
COMPUNCTION	10. Any uneasiness or hesitation about the rightness of an action
PESTILENCE	11. Something that is considered harmful, destructive, or evil
OVERWROUGHT	12. Extremely or excessively excited or agitated
HEARTH	13. The floor of a fireplace, usually of stone or brick
DIN	14. A loud, disturbing noise
VOID	15. An empty space; emptiness
FRAILTY	16. Moral weakness; liability to yield to temptation
REASSURED	17. Restored confidence to
PARRICIDE	18. A person who kills his own parent
SOOTHSAYER	19. Person who professes to foretell events, fortune-teller
EASE	20. Freedom from difficulty or great effort

Oedipus Vocabulary Fill In The Blanks 2

_____ 1. To regard or treat with reverence or respect

_____ 2. The utterance of a curse

_____ 3. Freedom from difficulty or great effort

_____ 4. Restored confidence to

_____ 5. To ask for humbly or earnestly, as by praying

_____ 6. The act of purifying by means of ceremony

_____ 7. An empty space; emptiness

_____ 8. A period of watchful attention maintained at night

_____ 9. Forced or drove out

_____ 10. Someone who releases people from captivity or bondage

_____ 11. Without rational basis

_____ 12. To thrive and prosper, especially at another's expense

_____ 13. A father's children

_____ 14. Female spirits who lived in forests, bodies of water, and other places outdoors

_____ 15. A tomb, grave, or burial place

_____ 16. Rude or impertinent behavior or speech

_____ 17. Moving or acting in an aimless or vague manner

_____ 18. A person who steers a ship

_____ 19. Moral weakness; liability to yield to temptation

_____ 20. A narrow strip of land, bordered on both sides by water, connecting two larger bodies of land

Oedipus Vocabulary Fill In The Blanks 2 Answer Key

VENERATE	1. To regard or treat with reverence or respect
MALEDICTION	2. The utterance of a curse
EASE	3. Freedom from difficulty or great effort
REASSURED	4. Restored confidence to
SUPPLICATION	5. To ask for humbly or earnestly, as by praying
LUSTRATION	6. The act of purifying by means of ceremony
VOID	7. An empty space; emptiness
VIGIL	8. A period of watchful attention maintained at night
EXPELLED	9. Forced or drove out
LIBERATOR	10. Someone who releases people from captivity or bondage
GROUNDLESS	11. Without rational basis
BATTENS	12. To thrive and prosper, especially at another's expense
SIRING	13. A father's children
NYMPHS	14. Female spirits who lived in forests, bodies of water, and other places outdoors
SEPULCHRE	15. A tomb, grave, or burial place
INSOLENCE	16. Rude or impertinent behavior or speech
MAUNDERING	17. Moving or acting in an aimless or vague manner
HELMSMAN	18. A person who steers a ship
FRAILTY	19. Moral weakness; liability to yield to temptation
ISTHMUS	20. A narrow strip of land, bordered on both sides by water, connecting two larger bodies of land

Oedipus Vocabulary Fill In The Blanks 3

1. Wise or judicious in practical affairs
2. To break up soil with a toll consisting of a heavy frame with sharp teeth
3. The killing of a king
4. An event indicating important things to come: fortune telling
5. Causing serious thoughts or a grave mood
6. A tomb, grave, or burial place
7. A person who kills his own parent
8. Something that is considered harmful, destructive, or evil
9. The utterance of a curse
10. Boldly shameless or impudent
11. Any authoritative proclamation or command
12. Widespread and high repute; fame
13. A person or thing that ruins or spoils
14. Weakened by old age; feeble
15. Those things claimed as exclusive rights
16. An enemy who lays siege to your positions
17. Anything greatly disliked or abhorred
18. Someone who releases people from captivity or bondage
19. Very unfortunate in condition or circumstances
20. To regard or treat with reverence or respect

Oedipus Vocabulary Fill In The Blanks 3 Answer Key

PRUDENT	1. Wise or judicious in practical affairs
HARROWED	2. To break up soil with a toll consisting of a heavy frame with sharp teeth
REGICIDE	3. The killing of a king
AUGURY	4. An event indicating important things to come: fortune telling
SOLEMN	5. Causing serious thoughts or a grave mood
SEPULCHRE	6. A tomb, grave, or burial place
PARRICIDE	7. A person who kills his own parent
PESTILENCE	8. Something that is considered harmful, destructive, or evil
MALEDICTION	9. The utterance of a curse
BRAZEN	10. Boldly shameless or impudent
EDICT	11. Any authoritative proclamation or command
RENOWN	12. Widespread and high repute; fame
BANE	13. A person or thing that ruins or spoils
DECREPIT	14. Weakened by old age; feeble
PERQUISITES	15. Those things claimed as exclusive rights
BESIEGER	16. An enemy who lays siege to your positions
ABOMINATION	17. Anything greatly disliked or abhorred
LIBERATOR	18. Someone who releases people from captivity or bondage
WRETCHED	19. Very unfortunate in condition or circumstances
VENERATE	20. To regard or treat with reverence or respect

Oedipus Vocabulary Fill In The Blanks 4

1. A group or clique within a larger group, party, or government
2. To take for granted, assume, or suppose
3. Being first in time; original
4. A person or thing that ruins or spoils
5. Any authoritative proclamation or command
6. Forced or drove out
7. Person who professes to foretell events, fortune-teller
8. Extremely or excessively excited or agitated
9. Those things claimed as exclusive rights
10. Moving or acting in an aimless or vague manner
11. A loud, disturbing noise
12. Caused keen irritation or bitter resentment
13. An enemy who lays siege to your positions
14. Boldly shameless or impudent
15. A cloth or sheet in which a corpse is wrapped for burial
16. Any uneasiness or hesitation about the rightness of an action
17. Any performance or ceremony regarded as absurd or false
18. Someone who releases people from captivity or bondage
19. A father's children
20. The act of purifying by means of ceremony

Oedipus Vocabulary Fill In The Blanks 4 Answer Key

FACTION	1. A group or clique within a larger group, party, or government
PRESUME	2. To take for granted, assume, or suppose
PRIMAL	3. Being first in time; original
BANE	4. A person or thing that ruins or spoils
EDICT	5. Any authoritative proclamation or command
EXPELLED	6. Forced or drove out
SOOTHSAYER	7. Person who professes to foretell events, fortune-teller
OVERWROUGHT	8. Extremely or excessively excited or agitated
PERQUISITES	9. Those things claimed as exclusive rights
MAUNDERING	10. Moving or acting in an aimless or vague manner
DIN	11. A loud, disturbing noise
RANKLED	12. Caused keen irritation or bitter resentment
BESIEGER	13. An enemy who lays siege to your positions
BRAZEN	14. Boldly shameless or impudent
SHROUD	15. A cloth or sheet in which a corpse is wrapped for burial
COMPUNCTION	16. Any uneasiness or hesitation about the rightness of an action
MUMMERY	17. Any performance or ceremony regarded as absurd or false
LIBERATOR	18. Someone who releases people from captivity or bondage
SIRING	19. A father's children
LUSTRATION	20. The act of purifying by means of ceremony

Oedipus Vocabulary Matching 1

___ 1. BESIEGER   A. Very unfortunate in condition or circumstances
___ 2. SUPPLICATION   B. Brilliant or gorgeous appearance
___ 3. EXPELLED   C. Any performance or ceremony regarded as absurd or false
___ 4. LIBERATOR   D. An enemy who lays siege to your positions
___ 5. PRUDENT   E. An event indicating important things to come: fortune telling
___ 6. WRETCHED   F. A person who steers a ship
___ 7. EXECRABLE   G. Extremely or excessively excited or agitated
___ 8. SCANT   H. A cloth or sheet in which a corpse is wrapped for burial
___ 9. HELMSMAN   I. Forced or drove out
___ 10. MALEDICTION   J. Weakened by old age; feeble
___ 11. BEGETTING   K. Fathering; siring
___ 12. DECREPIT   L. The utterance of a curse
___ 13. SPLENDOR   M. Wise or judicious in practical affairs
___ 14. SHROUD   N. Characteristic of or befitting an inferior person or thing
___ 15. CONTAGION   O. To treat slightly or inadequately
___ 16. RENOWN   P. Someone who releases people from captivity or bondage
___ 17. DIN   Q. The activity or business of pasturing livestock
___ 18. SOOTHSAYER   R. A loud, disturbing noise
___ 19. RANKLED   S. Those things claimed as exclusive rights
___ 20. PASTURAGE   T. Utterly detestable; abominable; very bad
___ 21. AUGURY   U. Person who professes to foretell events, fortune-teller
___ 22. BASENESS   V. Widespread and high repute; fame
___ 23. MUMMERY   W. Caused keen irritation or bitter resentment
___ 24. PERQUISITES   X. To ask for humbly or earnestly, as by praying
___ 25. OVERWROUGHT   Y. The means by which a contagious disease is transmitted

Oedipus Vocabulary Matching 1 Answer Key

D - 1.	BESIEGER	A. Very unfortunate in condition or circumstances
X - 2.	SUPPLICATION	B. Brilliant or gorgeous appearance
I - 3.	EXPELLED	C. Any performance or ceremony regarded as absurd or false
P - 4.	LIBERATOR	D. An enemy who lays siege to your positions
M - 5.	PRUDENT	E. An event indicating important things to come: fortune telling
A - 6.	WRETCHED	F. A person who steers a ship
T - 7.	EXECRABLE	G. Extremely or excessively excited or agitated
O - 8.	SCANT	H. A cloth or sheet in which a corpse is wrapped for burial
F - 9.	HELMSMAN	I. Forced or drove out
L - 10.	MALEDICTION	J. Weakened by old age; feeble
K - 11.	BEGETTING	K. Fathering; siring
J - 12.	DECREPIT	L. The utterance of a curse
B - 13.	SPLENDOR	M. Wise or judicious in practical affairs
H - 14.	SHROUD	N. Characteristic of or befitting an inferior person or thing
Y - 15.	CONTAGION	O. To treat slightly or inadequately
V - 16.	RENOWN	P. Someone who releases people from captivity or bondage
R - 17.	DIN	Q. The activity or business of pasturing livestock
U - 18.	SOOTHSAYER	R. A loud, disturbing noise
W - 19.	RANKLED	S. Those things claimed as exclusive rights
Q - 20.	PASTURAGE	T. Utterly detestable; abominable; very bad
E - 21.	AUGURY	U. Person who professes to foretell events, fortune-teller
N - 22.	BASENESS	V. Widespread and high repute; fame
C - 23.	MUMMERY	W. Caused keen irritation or bitter resentment
S - 24.	PERQUISITES	X. To ask for humbly or earnestly, as by praying
G - 25.	OVERWROUGHT	Y. The means by which a contagious disease is transmitted

Oedipus Vocabulary Matching 2

___ 1. PASTURAGE   A. Moral weakness; liability to yield to temptation
___ 2. DEFILEMENT   B. A father's children
___ 3. VENERATE   C. Person who professes to foretell events, fortune-teller
___ 4. MUMMERY   D. Fathering; siring
___ 5. PRIMAL   E. Restored confidence to
___ 6. CONTAGION   F. Relatively large decorative pins or clasps
___ 7. REASSURED   G. The utterance of a curse
___ 8. HELMSMAN   H. Very unfortunate in condition or circumstances
___ 9. SIRING   I. Widespread and high repute; fame
___10. BEGETTING   J. To take for granted, assume, or suppose
___11. HEARTH   K. Anything greatly disliked or abhorred
___12. BROOCHES   L. Any performance or ceremony regarded as absurd or false
___13. RENOWN   M. Being first in time; original
___14. BASENESS   N. A cloth or sheet in which a corpse is wrapped for burial
___15. MALEDICTION   O. To regard or treat with reverence or respect
___16. ABOMINATION   P. Wise or judicious in practical affairs
___17. WRETCHED   Q. To make foul, dirty, or unclean; pollute
___18. PARRICIDE   R. Any authoritative proclamation or command
___19. SHROUD   S. A person who kills his own parent
___20. EDICT   T. A person who steers a ship
___21. EASE   U. The activity or business of pasturing livestock
___22. PRUDENT   V. Characteristic of or befitting an inferior person or thing
___23. FRAILTY   W. The floor of a fireplace, usually of stone or brick
___24. PRESUME   X. The means by which a contagious disease is transmitted
___25. SOOTHSAYER   Y. Freedom from difficulty or great effort

Oedipus Vocabulary Matching 2 Answer Key

U - 1. PASTURAGE	A.	Moral weakness; liability to yield to temptation
Q - 2. DEFILEMENT	B.	A father's children
O - 3. VENERATE	C.	Person who professes to foretell events, fortune-teller
L - 4. MUMMERY	D.	Fathering; siring
M - 5. PRIMAL	E.	Restored confidence to
X - 6. CONTAGION	F.	Relatively large decorative pins or clasps
E - 7. REASSURED	G.	The utterance of a curse
T - 8. HELMSMAN	H.	Very unfortunate in condition or circumstances
B - 9. SIRING	I.	Widespread and high repute; fame
D - 10. BEGETTING	J.	To take for granted, assume, or suppose
W - 11. HEARTH	K.	Anything greatly disliked or abhorred
F - 12. BROOCHES	L.	Any performance or ceremony regarded as absurd or false
I - 13. RENOWN	M.	Being first in time; original
V - 14. BASENESS	N.	A cloth or sheet in which a corpse is wrapped for burial
G - 15. MALEDICTION	O.	To regard or treat with reverence or respect
K - 16. ABOMINATION	P.	Wise or judicious in practical affairs
H - 17. WRETCHED	Q.	To make foul, dirty, or unclean; pollute
S - 18. PARRICIDE	R.	Any authoritative proclamation or command
N - 19. SHROUD	S.	A person who kills his own parent
R - 20. EDICT	T.	A person who steers a ship
Y - 21. EASE	U.	The activity or business of pasturing livestock
P - 22. PRUDENT	V.	Characteristic of or befitting an inferior person or thing
A - 23. FRAILTY	W.	The floor of a fireplace, usually of stone or brick
J - 24. PRESUME	X.	The means by which a contagious disease is transmitted
C - 25. SOOTHSAYER	Y.	Freedom from difficulty or great effort

Oedipus Vocabulary Matching 3

___ 1. HEARTH   A. One who is rejected or discarded
___ 2. DECREPIT   B. A person who kills his own parent
___ 3. DIN   C. To ask for humbly or earnestly, as by praying
___ 4. CONTAGION   D. A loud, disturbing noise
___ 5. BESIEGER   E. Those things claimed as exclusive rights
___ 6. SIRING   F. Freedom from difficulty or great effort
___ 7. SUPPLICATION   G. A person who steers a ship
___ 8. BROOCHES   H. An enemy who lays siege to your positions
___ 9. HELMSMAN   I. To treat slightly or inadequately
___10. SCANT   J. To break up soil with a toll consisting of a heavy frame with sharp teeth
___11. LIBERATOR   K. Brilliant or gorgeous appearance
___12. SOOTHSAYER   L. Any performance or ceremony regarded as absurd or false
___13. SPLENDOR   M. Relatively large decorative pins or clasps
___14. SOLEMN   N. Any uneasiness or hesitation about the rightness of an action
___15. MUMMERY   O. Anything greatly disliked or abhorred
___16. PERQUISITES   P. Extremely or excessively excited or agitated
___17. OVERWROUGHT   Q. Something that is considered harmful, destructive, or evil
___18. PASTURAGE   R. Person who professes to foretell events, fortune-teller
___19. ABOMINATION   S. Weakened by old age; feeble
___20. EASE   T. The activity or business of pasturing livestock
___21. PESTILENCE   U. Someone who releases people from captivity or bondage
___22. HARROWED   V. Causing serious thoughts or a grave mood
___23. COMPUNCTION   W. A father's children
___24. OUTCAST   X. The means by which a contagious disease is transmitted
___25. PARRICIDE   Y. The floor of a fireplace, usually of stone or brick

Oedipus Vocabulary Matching 3 Answer Key

Y - 1.	HEARTH	A.	One who is rejected or discarded
S - 2.	DECREPIT	B.	A person who kills his own parent
D - 3.	DIN	C.	To ask for humbly or earnestly, as by praying
X - 4.	CONTAGION	D.	A loud, disturbing noise
H - 5.	BESIEGER	E.	Those things claimed as exclusive rights
W - 6.	SIRING	F.	Freedom from difficulty or great effort
C - 7.	SUPPLICATION	G.	A person who steers a ship
M - 8.	BROOCHES	H.	An enemy who lays siege to your positions
G - 9.	HELMSMAN	I.	To treat slightly or inadequately
I - 10.	SCANT	J.	To break up soil with a toll consisting of a heavy frame with sharp teeth
U - 11.	LIBERATOR	K.	Brilliant or gorgeous appearance
R - 12.	SOOTHSAYER	L.	Any performance or ceremony regarded as absurd or false
K - 13.	SPLENDOR	M.	Relatively large decorative pins or clasps
V - 14.	SOLEMN	N.	Any uneasiness or hesitation about the rightness of an action
L - 15.	MUMMERY	O.	Anything greatly disliked or abhorred
E - 16.	PERQUISITES	P.	Extremely or excessively excited or agitated
P - 17.	OVERWROUGHT	Q.	Something that is considered harmful, destructive, or evil
T - 18.	PASTURAGE	R.	Person who professes to foretell events, fortune-teller
O - 19.	ABOMINATION	S.	Weakened by old age; feeble
F - 20.	EASE	T.	The activity or business of pasturing livestock
Q - 21.	PESTILENCE	U.	Someone who releases people from captivity or bondage
J - 22.	HARROWED	V.	Causing serious thoughts or a grave mood
N - 23.	COMPUNCTION	W.	A father's children
A - 24.	OUTCAST	X.	The means by which a contagious disease is transmitted
B - 25.	PARRICIDE	Y.	The floor of a fireplace, usually of stone or brick

Oedipus Vocabulary Matching 4

___ 1. SOOTHSAYER	A. A person who steers a ship
___ 2. BANE	B. Being first in time; original
___ 3. HELMSMAN	C. Anything greatly disliked or abhorred
___ 4. SCANT	D. Something that is considered harmful, destructive, or evil
___ 5. OUTCAST	E. To take for granted, assume, or suppose
___ 6. ABOMINATION	F. Person who professes to foretell events, fortune-teller
___ 7. PRIMAL	G. A group or clique within a larger group, party, or government
___ 8. SIRING	H. To regard or treat with reverence or respect
___ 9. SPLENDOR	I. A father's children
___10. HEARTH	J. The floor of a fireplace, usually of stone or brick
___11. MAUNDERING	K. A person or thing that ruins or spoils
___12. AUGURY	L. Moving or acting in an aimless or vague manner
___13. SHROUD	M. Female spirits who lived in forests, bodies of water, and other places outdoors
___14. VENERATE	N. Fathering; siring
___15. NYMPHS	O. To turn aside; evade or dodge
___16. VOID	P. Those things claimed as exclusive rights
___17. PARRY	Q. A tomb, grave, or burial place
___18. PRESUME	R. An event indicating important things to come: fortune telling
___19. DEFILEMENT	S. An empty space; emptiness
___20. SEPULCHRE	T. One who is rejected or discarded
___21. LIBERATOR	U. Brilliant or gorgeous appearance
___22. FACTION	V. Someone who releases people from captivity or bondage
___23. PESTILENCE	W. To treat slightly or inadequately
___24. BEGETTING	X. To make foul, dirty, or unclean; pollute
___25. PERQUISITES	Y. A cloth or sheet in which a corpse is wrapped for burial

Oedipus Vocabulary Matching 4 Answer Key

F - 1. SOOTHSAYER	A.	A person who steers a ship
K - 2. BANE	B.	Being first in time; original
A - 3. HELMSMAN	C.	Anything greatly disliked or abhorred
W - 4. SCANT	D.	Something that is considered harmful, destructive, or evil
T - 5. OUTCAST	E.	To take for granted, assume, or suppose
C - 6. ABOMINATION	F.	Person who professes to foretell events, fortune-teller
B - 7. PRIMAL	G.	A group or clique within a larger group, party, or government
I - 8. SIRING	H.	To regard or treat with reverence or respect
U - 9. SPLENDOR	I.	A father's children
J - 10. HEARTH	J.	The floor of a fireplace, usually of stone or brick
L - 11. MAUNDERING	K.	A person or thing that ruins or spoils
R - 12. AUGURY	L.	Moving or acting in an aimless or vague manner
Y - 13. SHROUD	M.	Female spirits who lived in forests, bodies of water, and other places outdoors
H - 14. VENERATE	N.	Fathering; siring
M - 15. NYMPHS	O.	To turn aside; evade or dodge
S - 16. VOID	P.	Those things claimed as exclusive rights
O - 17. PARRY	Q.	A tomb, grave, or burial place
E - 18. PRESUME	R.	An event indicating important things to come: fortune telling
X - 19. DEFILEMENT	S.	An empty space; emptiness
Q - 20. SEPULCHRE	T.	One who is rejected or discarded
V - 21. LIBERATOR	U.	Brilliant or gorgeous appearance
G - 22. FACTION	V.	Someone who releases people from captivity or bondage
D - 23. PESTILENCE	W.	To treat slightly or inadequately
N - 24. BEGETTING	X.	To make foul, dirty, or unclean; pollute
P - 25. PERQUISITES	Y.	A cloth or sheet in which a corpse is wrapped for burial

Oedipus Vocabulary Magic Squares 1

Match the definition with the vocabulary word. Put your answers in the magic squares below. When your answers are correct, all columns and rows will add to the same number.

A. DEFILEMENT
B. MUMMERY
C. ABOMINATION
D. VIGIL
E. EASE
F. FRAILTY
G. OVERWROUGHT
H. HELMSMAN
I. FACTION
J. PERQUISITES
K. HARROWED
L. COMPUNCTION
M. SUPPLIANT
N. GROUNDLESS
O. RENOWN
P. DECREPIT

1. Any performance or ceremony regarded as absurd or false
2. Extremely or excessively excited or agitated
3. To break up soil with a toll consisting of a heavy frame with sharp teeth
4. Without rational basis
5. One who asks humbly and earnestly
6. Any uneasiness or hesitation about the rightness of an action
7. A person who steers a ship
8. To make foul, dirty, or unclean; pollute
9. Weakened by old age; feeble
10. A group or clique within a larger group, party, or government
11. Freedom from difficulty or great effort
12. A period of watchful attention maintained at night
13. Anything greatly disliked or abhorred
14. Moral weakness; liability to yield to temptation
15. Those things claimed as exclusive rights
16. Widespread and high repute; fame

A=	B=	C=	D=
E=	F=	G=	H=
I=	J=	K=	L=
M=	N=	O=	P=

Oedipus Vocabulary Magic Squares 1 Answer Key

Match the definition with the vocabulary word. Put your answers in the magic squares below. When your answers are correct, all columns and rows will add to the same number.

A. DEFILEMENT
B. MUMMERY
C. ABOMINATION
D. VIGIL
E. EASE
F. FRAILTY
G. OVERWROUGHT
H. HELMSMAN
I. FACTION
J. PERQUISITES
K. HARROWED
L. COMPUNCTION
M. SUPPLIANT
N. GROUNDLESS
O. RENOWN
P. DECREPIT

1. Any performance or ceremony regarded as absurd or false
2. Extremely or excessively excited or agitated
3. To break up soil with a toll consisting of a heavy frame with sharp teeth
4. Without rational basis
5. One who asks humbly and earnestly
6. Any uneasiness or hesitation about the rightness of an action
7. A person who steers a ship
8. To make foul, dirty, or unclean; pollute
9. Weakened by old age; feeble
10. A group or clique within a larger group, party, or government
11. Freedom from difficulty or great effort
12. A period of watchful attention maintained at night
13. Anything greatly disliked or abhorred
14. Moral weakness; liability to yield to temptation
15. Those things claimed as exclusive rights
16. Widespread and high repute; fame

A=8	B=1	C=13	D=12
E=11	F=14	G=2	H=7
I=10	J=15	K=3	L=6
M=5	N=4	O=16	P=9

Oedipus Vocabulary Magic Squares 2

Match the definition with the vocabulary word. Put your answers in the magic squares below. When your answers are correct, all columns and rows will add to the same number.

A. HEARTH
B. BROOCHES
C. EXPELLED
D. PERQUISITES
E. SCANT
F. PARRICIDE
G. SIRING
H. RENOWN
I. SUPPLICATION
J. MAUNDERING
K. VENERATE
L. BANE
M. SOOTHSAYER
N. EXECRABLE
O. REGICIDE
P. SEPULCHRE

1. A person who kills his own parent
2. To ask for humbly or earnestly, as by praying
3. The killing of a king
4. Those things claimed as exclusive rights
5. Person who professes to foretell events, fortune-teller
6. Relatively large decorative pins or clasps
7. Widespread and high repute; fame
8. To regard or treat with reverence or respect
9. Forced or drove out
10. A tomb, grave, or burial place
11. Moving or acting in an aimless or vague manner
12. To treat slightly or inadequately
13. A person or thing that ruins or spoils
14. A father's children
15. The floor of a fireplace, usually of stone or brick
16. Utterly detestable; abominable; very bad

A=	B=	C=	D=
E=	F=	G=	H=
I=	J=	K=	L=
M=	N=	O=	P=

Oedipus Vocabulary Magic Squares 2 Answer Key

Match the definition with the vocabulary word. Put your answers in the magic squares below. When your answers are correct, all columns and rows will add to the same number.

A. HEARTH
B. BROOCHES
C. EXPELLED
D. PERQUISITES
E. SCANT
F. PARRICIDE
G. SIRING
H. RENOWN
I. SUPPLICATION
J. MAUNDERING
K. VENERATE
L. BANE
M. SOOTHSAYER
N. EXECRABLE
O. REGICIDE
P. SEPULCHRE

1. A person who kills his own parent
2. To ask for humbly or earnestly, as by praying
3. The killing of a king
4. Those things claimed as exclusive rights
5. Person who professes to foretell events, fortune-teller
6. Relatively large decorative pins or clasps
7. Widespread and high repute; fame
8. To regard or treat with reverence or respect
9. Forced or drove out
10. A tomb, grave, or burial place
11. Moving or acting in an aimless or vague manner
12. To treat slightly or inadequately
13. A person or thing that ruins or spoils
14. A father's children
15. The floor of a fireplace, usually of stone or brick
16. Utterly detestable; abominable; very bad

A=15	B=6	C=9	D=4
E=12	F=1	G=14	H=7
I=2	J=11	K=8	L=13
M=5	N=16	O=3	P=10

Oedipus Vocabulary Magic Squares 3

Match the definition with the vocabulary word. Put your answers in the magic squares below. When your answers are correct, all columns and rows will add to the same number.

A. PESTILENCE
B. MAUNDERING
C. REASSURED
D. BROOCHES
E. PRIMAL
F. REGICIDE
G. DEFILEMENT
H. BESIEGER
I. AUGURY
J. GROUNDLESS
K. FRAILTY
L. VENERATE
M. SPLENDOR
N. PRUDENT
O. BANE
P. ABOMINATION

1. A person or thing that ruins or spoils
2. Without rational basis
3. An enemy who lays siege to your positions
4. Something that is considered harmful, destructive, or evil
5. Relatively large decorative pins or clasps
6. Being first in time; original
7. Moral weakness; liability to yield to temptation
8. Wise or judicious in practical affairs
9. The killing of a king
10. Restored confidence to
11. Brilliant or gorgeous appearance
12. To regard or treat with reverence or respect
13. An event indicating important things to come: fortune telling
14. Anything greatly disliked or abhorred
15. Moving or acting in an aimless or vague manner
16. To make foul, dirty, or unclean; pollute

A=	B=	C=	D=
E=	F=	G=	H=
I=	J=	K=	L=
M=	N=	O=	P=

Oedipus Vocabulary Magic Squares 3 Answer Key

Match the definition with the vocabulary word. Put your answers in the magic squares below. When your answers are correct, all columns and rows will add to the same number.

A. PESTILENCE
B. MAUNDERING
C. REASSURED
D. BROOCHES
E. PRIMAL
F. REGICIDE
G. DEFILEMENT
H. BESIEGER
I. AUGURY
J. GROUNDLESS
K. FRAILTY
L. VENERATE
M. SPLENDOR
N. PRUDENT
O. BANE
P. ABOMINATION

1. A person or thing that ruins or spoils
2. Without rational basis
3. An enemy who lays siege to your positions
4. Something that is considered harmful, destructive, or evil
5. Relatively large decorative pins or clasps
6. Being first in time; original
7. Moral weakness; liability to yield to temptation
8. Wise or judicious in practical affairs
9. The killing of a king
10. Restored confidence to
11. Brilliant or gorgeous appearance
12. To regard or treat with reverence or respect
13. An event indicating important things to come: fortune telling
14. Anything greatly disliked or abhorred
15. Moving or acting in an aimless or vague manner
16. To make foul, dirty, or unclean; pollute

A=4	B=15	C=10	D=5
E=6	F=9	G=16	H=3
I=13	J=2	K=7	L=12
M=11	N=8	O=1	P=14

Oedipus Vocabulary Magic Squares 4

Match the definition with the vocabulary word. Put your answers in the magic squares below. When your answers are correct, all columns and rows will add to the same number.

A. DEFILEMENT
B. BATTENS
C. EXECRABLE
D. LUSTRATION
E. NYMPHS
F. VOID
G. BESIEGER
H. CONTAGION
I. RANKLED
J. REGICIDE
K. PRUDENT
L. ISTHMUS
M. ABOMINATION
N. HEARTH
O. FRAILTY
P. BASENESS

1. Utterly detestable; abominable; very bad
2. The killing of a king
3. An empty space; emptiness
4. Moral weakness; liability to yield to temptation
5. Characteristic of or befitting an inferior person or thing
6. Female spirits who lived in forests, bodies of water, and other places outdoors
7. Caused keen irritation or bitter resentment
8. The act of purifying by means of ceremony
9. Anything greatly disliked or abhorred
10. The means by which a contagious disease is transmitted
11. A narrow strip of land, bordered on both sides by water, connecting two larger bodies of land
12. To make foul, dirty, or unclean; pollute
13. To thrive and prosper, especially at another's expense
14. Wise or judicious in practical affairs
15. An enemy who lays siege to your positions
16. The floor of a fireplace, usually of stone or brick

A=	B=	C=	D=
E=	F=	G=	H=
I=	J=	K=	L=
M=	N=	O=	P=

Oedipus Vocabulary Magic Squares 4 Answer Key

Match the definition with the vocabulary word. Put your answers in the magic squares below. When your answers are correct, all columns and rows will add to the same number.

A. DEFILEMENT
B. BATTENS
C. EXECRABLE
D. LUSTRATION
E. NYMPHS
F. VOID
G. BESIEGER
H. CONTAGION
I. RANKLED
J. REGICIDE
K. PRUDENT
L. ISTHMUS
M. ABOMINATION
N. HEARTH
O. FRAILTY
P. BASENESS

1. Utterly detestable; abominable; very bad
2. The killing of a king
3. An empty space; emptiness
4. Moral weakness; liability to yield to temptation
5. Characteristic of or befitting an inferior person or thing
6. Female spirits who lived in forests, bodies of water, and other places outdoors
7. Caused keen irritation or bitter resentment
8. The act of purifying by means of ceremony
9. Anything greatly disliked or abhorred
10. The means by which a contagious disease is transmitted
11. A narrow strip of land, bordered on both sides by water, connecting two larger bodies of land
12. To make foul, dirty, or unclean; pollute
13. To thrive and prosper, especially at another's expense
14. Wise or judicious in practical affairs
15. An enemy who lays siege to your positions
16. The floor of a fireplace, usually of stone or brick

A=12	B=13	C=1	D=8
E=6	F=3	G=15	H=10
I=7	J=2	K=14	L=11
M=9	N=16	O=4	P=5

Oedipus Vocabulary Word Search 1

```
P A R R I C I D E C R E P I T P B B V N
R A S E Z L W N N X X E J V K R A A E R
I F S P G D Q Z X M E N N W G U T S N L
M A N T L I N Y M A I C J O K D T E E E
A C M Y U E C Q L U F S R O W E E N R J
L T B U M R N I L N S H T A U N N E A V
G I V R M P A D D D O R B H B T S S T J
T O N Q E M H G O E O O W R M L C S E V
L N V S Q A E S E R T U M R O U E A N F
S W P X O Q S R Z I H D K W A O S Y S B
S E Y A F L H S Y N S Z S J P N C Q J T
H I P M R S E F U G A G V H E G K H Z F
X E R U F R B N S R Y S X O D H D L E M
F R A I L T Y R C P E R Q U I S I T E S
S X C R N C D G A E R D P P C D N R W D
R J Y N T G H Z N Z Y V W Y T X E L Q T
V I G I L H K R T H E L M S M A N A J B
W R E T C H E D E C O N T A G I O N S C
E N Q U I R Y S O L E M N A U G U R Y E
```

- A cloth or sheet in which a corpse is wrapped for burial (6)
- A father's children (6)
- A group or clique within a larger group, party, or government (7)
- A loud, disturbing noise (3)
- A narrow strip of land, bordered on both sides by water, connecting two larger bodies of land (7)
- A period of watchful attention maintained at night (5)
- A person or thing that ruins or spoils (4)
- A person who kills his own parent (9)
- A person who steers a ship (8)
- A seeking or request for truth, information, or knowledge (7)
- A tomb, grave, or burial place (9)
- An empty space; emptiness (4)
- An event indicating important things to come: fortune telling (6)
- Any authoritative proclamation or command (5)
- Any performance or ceremony regarded as absurd or false (7)
- Being first in time; original (6)
- Boldly shameless or impudent (6)
- Brilliant or gorgeous appearance (8)
- Caused keen irritation or bitter resentment (7)
- Causing serious thoughts or a grave mood (6)
- Characteristic of or befitting an inferior person or thing (8)
- Female spirits who lived in forests, bodies of water, and other places outdoors (6)
- Freedom from difficulty or great effort (4)
- Moral weakness; liability to yield to temptation (7)
- Moving or acting in an aimless or vague manner (10)
- One who is rejected or discarded (7)
- Person who professes to foretell events, fortune-teller (10)
- Relatively large decorative pins or clasps (8)
- Restored confidence to (9)
- Rude or impertinent behavior or speech (9)
- The activity or business of pasturing livestock (9)
- The floor of a fireplace, usually of stone or brick (6)
- The killing of a king (8)
- The means by which a contagious disease is transmitted (9)
- Those things claimed as exclusive rights (11)
- To regard or treat with reverence or respect (8)
- To thrive and prosper, especially at another's expense (7)
- To treat slightly or inadequately (5)
- To turn aside; evade or dodge (5)
- Utterly detestable; abominable; very bad (9)
- Very unfortunate in condition or circumstances (8)
- Weakened by old age; feeble (8)
- Widespread and high repute; fame (6)
- Wise or judicious in practical affairs (7)

Oedipus Vocabulary Word Search 1 Answer Key

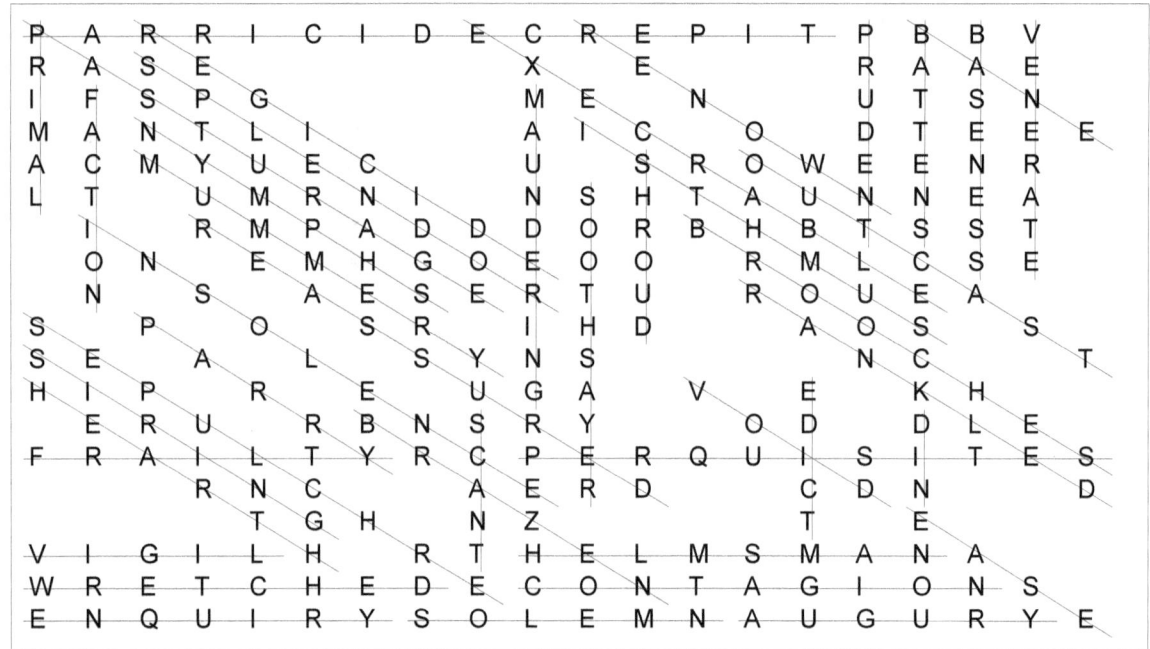

A cloth or sheet in which a corpse is wrapped for burial (6)
A father's children (6)
A group or clique within a larger group, party, or government (7)
A loud, disturbing noise (3)
A narrow strip of land, bordered on both sides by water, connecting two larger bodies of land (7)
A period of watchful attention maintained at night (5)
A person or thing that ruins or spoils (4)
A person who kills his own parent (9)
A person who steers a ship (8)
A seeking or request for truth, information, or knowledge (7)
A tomb, grave, or burial place (9)
An empty space; emptiness (4)
An event indicating important things to come: fortune telling (6)
Any authoritative proclamation or command (5)
Any performance or ceremony regarded as absurd or false (7)
Being first in time; original (6)
Boldly shameless or impudent (6)
Brilliant or gorgeous appearance (8)
Caused keen irritation or bitter resentment (7)
Causing serious thoughts or a grave mood (6)
Characteristic of or befitting an inferior person or thing (8)

Female spirits who lived in forests, bodies of water, and other places outdoors (6)
Freedom from difficulty or great effort (4)
Moral weakness; liability to yield to temptation (7)
Moving or acting in an aimless or vague manner (10)
One who is rejected or discarded (7)
Person who professes to foretell events, fortune-teller (10)
Relatively large decorative pins or clasps (8)
Restored confidence to (9)
Rude or impertinent behavior or speech (9)
The activity or business of pasturing livestock (9)
The floor of a fireplace, usually of stone or brick (6)
The killing of a king (8)
The means by which a contagious disease is transmitted (9)
Those things claimed as exclusive rights (11)
To regard or treat with reverence or respect (8)
To thrive and prosper, especially at another's expense (7)
To treat slightly or inadequately (5)
To turn aside; evade or dodge (5)
Utterly detestable; abominable; very bad (9)
Very unfortunate in condition or circumstances (8)
Weakened by old age; feeble (8)
Widespread and high repute; fame (6)
Wise or judicious in practical affairs (7)

Oedipus Vocabulary Word Search 2

```
L I B E R A T O R P E R Q U I S I T E S
P B D R D E N Y O P R U D E N T A S X Z
R E E F A X G N U W R I R R R E U O S M
E S F N R Z C I T R J K M N X X G O E Z
S I I Z Q A E B C C F V R A W E U T P D
U E S B U I N A I B R E W L C R H U N
M G E X J S I L S L D A A R V R Y S L D
E E M L V V K R T V K E S N G A B A C W
B R E R W D Z P Y Y X F S E K B A Y H R
C A N V E I N S E G F B U M N L N E R M
T S T H I N N P A S T U R A G E E R E M
M H H T E G O Y G U T T E O S D S D V S
G R E S E A I W M P M I D I O I G S O S
S O L E M N R L N P L U L E S C R K I V
J U M Y N B S T R L H S M E A T H I D T
M D S V R T V W H I R S C M N S H E N B
C P M P A R R Y B A V Z Z A E C E M S G
Z D A F A B O M I N A T I O N R E N U V
C O N T A G I O N T L L B Z F T Y Z V S
```

A cloth or sheet in which a corpse is wrapped for burial (6)
A father's children (6)
A loud, disturbing noise (3)
A narrow strip of land, bordered on both sides by water, connecting two larger bodies of land (7)
A period of watchful attention maintained at night (5)
A person or thing that ruins or spoils (4)
A person who steers a ship (8)
A seeking or request for truth, information, or knowledge (7)
A tomb, grave, or burial place (9)
An empty space; emptiness (4)
An enemy who lays siege to your positions (8)
An event indicating important things to come: fortune telling (6)
Any authoritative proclamation or command (5)
Any performance or ceremony regarded as absurd or false (7)
Anything greatly disliked or abhorred (11)
Being first in time; original (6)
Boldly shameless or impudent (6)
Caused keen irritation or bitter resentment (7)
Causing serious thoughts or a grave mood (6)
Characteristic of or befitting an inferior person or thing (8)
Female spirits who lived in forests, bodies of water, and other places outdoors (6)

Freedom from difficulty or great effort (4)
Moral weakness; liability to yield to temptation (7)
One who asks humbly and earnestly (9)
One who is rejected or discarded (7)
Person who professes to foretell events, fortune-teller (10)
Relatively large decorative pins or clasps (8)
Restored confidence to (9)
Someone who releases people from captivity or bondage (9)
Something that is considered harmful, destructive, or evil (10)
The activity or business of pasturing livestock (9)
The floor of a fireplace, usually of stone or brick (6)
The killing of a king (8)
The means by which a contagious disease is transmitted (9)
Those things claimed as exclusive rights (11)
To make foul, dirty, or unclean; pollute (10)
To take for granted, assume, or suppose (7)
To thrive and prosper, especially at another's expense (7)
To treat slightly or inadequately (5)
To turn aside; evade or dodge (5)
Utterly detestable; abominable; very bad (9)
Widespread and high repute; fame (6)
Wise or judicious in practical affairs (7)

Oedipus Vocabulary Word Search 2 Answer Key

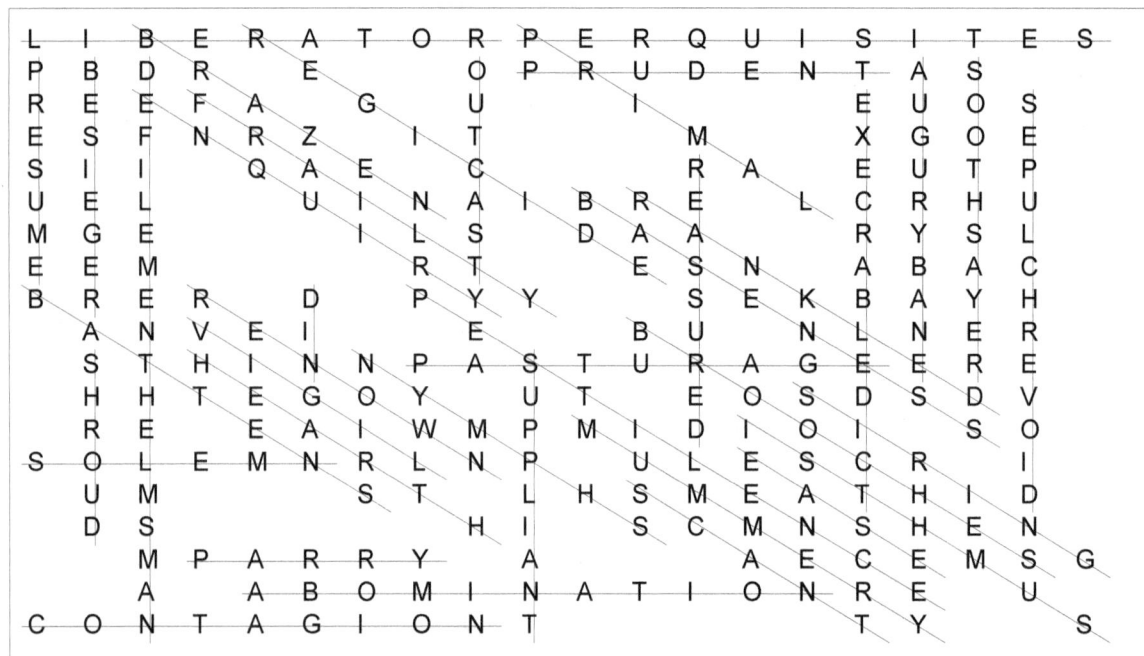

- A cloth or sheet in which a corpse is wrapped for burial (6)
- A father's children (6)
- A loud, disturbing noise (3)
- A narrow strip of land, bordered on both sides by water, connecting two larger bodies of land (7)
- A period of watchful attention maintained at night (5)
- A person or thing that ruins or spoils (4)
- A person who steers a ship (8)
- A seeking or request for truth, information, or knowledge (7)
- A tomb, grave, or burial place (9)
- An empty space; emptiness (4)
- An enemy who lays siege to your positions (8)
- An event indicating important things to come: fortune telling (6)
- Any authoritative proclamation or command (5)
- Any performance or ceremony regarded as absurd or false (7)
- Anything greatly disliked or abhorred (11)
- Being first in time; original (6)
- Boldly shameless or impudent (6)
- Caused keen irritation or bitter resentment (7)
- Causing serious thoughts or a grave mood (6)
- Characteristic of or befitting an inferior person or thing (8)
- Female spirits who lived in forests, bodies of water, and other places outdoors (6)
- Freedom from difficulty or great effort (4)
- Moral weakness; liability to yield to temptation (7)
- One who asks humbly and earnestly (9)
- One who is rejected or discarded (7)
- Person who professes to foretell events, fortune-teller (10)
- Relatively large decorative pins or clasps (8)
- Restored confidence to (9)
- Someone who releases people from captivity or bondage (9)
- Something that is considered harmful, destructive, or evil (10)
- The activity or business of pasturing livestock (9)
- The floor of a fireplace, usually of stone or brick (6)
- The killing of a king (8)
- The means by which a contagious disease is transmitted (9)
- Those things claimed as exclusive rights (11)
- To make foul, dirty, or unclean; pollute (10)
- To take for granted, assume, or suppose (7)
- To thrive and prosper, especially at another's expense (7)
- To treat slightly or inadequately (5)
- To turn aside; evade or dodge (5)
- Utterly detestable; abominable; very bad (9)
- Widespread and high repute; fame (6)
- Wise or judicious in practical affairs (7)

Oedipus Vocabulary Word Search 3

```
I  H  V  E  H  A  R  R  O  W  E  D  M  U  M  M  E  R  Y  B
S  N  O  X  S  S  E  F  A  C  T  I  O  N  S  A  R  E  F  S
T  S  I  P  O  H  G  B  R  O  O  C  H  E  S  U  T  A  R  V
H  E  D  E  O  R  I  P  R  U  D  E  N  T  M  N  P  S  A  X
M  P  E  L  T  O  C  C  H  M  B  S  N  R  J  D  A  S  I  N
U  U  C  L  H  U  I  O  P  Y  A  E  P  M  S  E  R  U  L  M
S  L  R  E  S  D  D  N  H  X  R  L  S  L  M  R  R  R  T  X
H  C  E  D  A  M  E  T  N  W  C  G  E  I  E  I  Y  E  Y  Y
D  H  P  D  Y  T  Y  A  S  Q  N  S  V  D  E  N  C  D  Z  N
P  R  I  Q  E  K  Z  G  P  X  B  S  E  R  I  G  D  J  B  R
E  E  T  V  R  V  D  I  R  Y  T  N  N  E  S  C  E  O  L  G
R  Q  S  L  F  I  B  O  E  P  S  S  E  N  C  Y  T  R  R  X
Q  P  C  T  J  G  N  N  S  C  A  C  R  O  H  K  X  I  Z  R
U  G  B  Y  I  L  Y  U  Q  H  S  A  W  Y  B  R  J  O  A
I  R  F  H  E  L  M  S  M  A  N  C  T  N  S  O  L  E  M  N
S  O  A  O  W  E  E  Z  E  P  R  S  E  U  T  W  M  B  S  K
I  U  Y  U  N  N  Z  N  M  E  H  R  Y  I  R  Z  B  A  U  L
T  N  P  T  G  Q  S  F  C  X  V  S  V  N  H  A  E  T  P  E
E  D  I  C  T  U  B  A  S  E  N  E  S  S  E  P  G  T  P  D
S  L  S  A  R  I  R  D  N  C  A  S  L  O  A  R  E  E  L  Y
J  E  I  S  N  R  A  Y  V  R  J  S  G  L  R  I  T  N  I  R
M  S  R  T  Q  Y  Z  P  G  A  V  P  E  E  T  M  T  S  A  M
R  S  I  Q  D  L  E  Q  J  B  A  N  E  N  H  A  I  M  N  Q
B  G  N  H  S  I  N  X  J  L  J  N  D  C  G  L  N  P  T  K
B  W  G  Y  J  T  N  W  R  E  T  C  H  E  D  T  G  V  T  T
```

AUGURY	EASE	INSOLENCE	PRESUME	SOLEMN
BANE	EDICT	ISTHMUS	PRIMAL	SOOTHSAYER
BASENESS	ENQUIRY	MALEDICTION	PRUDENT	SPLENDOR
BATTENS	EXECRABLE	MAUNDERING	RANKLED	SUPPLIANT
BEGETTING	EXPELLED	MUMMERY	REASSURED	VENERATE
BESIEGER	FACTION	NYMPHS	REGICIDE	VIGIL
BRAZEN	FRAILTY	OUTCAST	RENOWN	VOID
BROOCHES	GROUNDLESS	PARRY	SCANT	WRETCHED
CONTAGION	HARROWED	PASTURAGE	SEPULCHRE	
DECREPIT	HEARTH	PERQUISITES	SHROUD	
DIN	HELMSMAN	PESTILENCE	SIRING	

Oedipus Vocabulary Word Search 3 Answer Key

AUGURY	EASE	INSOLENCE	PRESUME	SOLEMN
BANE	EDICT	ISTHMUS	PRIMAL	SOOTHSAYER
BASENESS	ENQUIRY	MALEDICTION	PRUDENT	SPLENDOR
BATTENS	EXECRABLE	MAUNDERING	RANKLED	SUPPLIANT
BEGETTING	EXPELLED	MUMMERY	REASSURED	VENERATE
BESIEGER	FACTION	NYMPHS	REGICIDE	VIGIL
BRAZEN	FRAILTY	OUTCAST	RENOWN	VOID
BROOCHES	GROUNDLESS	PARRY	SCANT	WRETCHED
CONTAGION	HARROWED	PASTURAGE	SEPULCHRE	
DECREPIT	HEARTH	PERQUISITES	SHROUD	
DIN	HELMSMAN	PESTILENCE	SIRING	

Oedipus Vocabulary Word Search 4

```
S P L E N D O R E G I C I D E B M H V W
I E G R O U N D L E S S R E I R X A E R
R S P A S T U R A G E R E A S O M R N C
I T B U D E C R E P I T N S T O H R E Y
N I E P L Y P P F N H B O E H C P O R H
G L S R D C R L E A Q Q W F M H I W A J
H E I U T W H N X R C U N J U E N E T B
P N E D K D T R S J Q T I R S S S D E N
X C G E L Y J N E P B U I R B Y O S R D
O E E N U T G Z A R A S I O Y J L G Z V
E U R T S F N J B I T O O S N W E C Y B
S D T Y T R R L O M T O N L I C N X C D
U B I C R N D A M A E T Y S E T C P B C
P A S C A N T H I L N H M U M M E R Y F
P S H O T S B E N L S S P P A B N S R X
L E R N I E T A A P T A H P U R W P E Z
I N O T O X H R T A R Y S L N A R R A L
A E U A N P B T I R A E P I D Z E E S M
N S D G D E A H O R N R H C E E T S S X
T S A I I L N V N I K N C A R N C U U L
P R U O N L E S O C L G V T I F H M R K
A D G N M E V N D I E C Z I N Y E E E V
R R U P T D G Y M D D B B O G L D N D S
R G R G H V B E G E T T I N G I Z Z B K
Y Q Y F N Z H E L M S M A N G B L Y H C
```

ABOMINATION	DIN	INSOLENCE	PESTILENCE	SIRING
AUGURY	EASE	ISTHMUS	PRESUME	SOLEMN
BANE	EDICT	LUSTRATION	PRIMAL	SOOTHSAYER
BASENESS	ENQUIRY	MAUNDERING	PRUDENT	SPLENDOR
BATTENS	EXPELLED	MUMMERY	RANKLED	SUPPLIANT
BEGETTING	FACTION	NYMPHS	REASSURED	SUPPLICATION
BESIEGER	FRAILTY	OUTCAST	REGICIDE	VENERATE
BRAZEN	GROUNDLESS	PARRICIDE	RENOWN	VIGIL
BROOCHES	HARROWED	PARRY	SCANT	VOID
CONTAGION	HEARTH	PASTURAGE	SEPULCHRE	WRETCHED
DECREPIT	HELMSMAN	PERQUISITES	SHROUD	

Copyrighted

Oedipus Vocabulary Word Search 4 Answer Key

ABOMINATION	DIN	INSOLENCE	PESTILENCE	SIRING
AUGURY	EASE	ISTHMUS	PRESUME	SOLEMN
BANE	EDICT	LUSTRATION	PRIMAL	SOOTHSAYER
BASENESS	ENQUIRY	MAUNDERING	PRUDENT	SPLENDOR
BATTENS	EXPELLED	MUMMERY	RANKLED	SUPPLIANT
BEGETTING	FACTION	NYMPHS	REASSURED	SUPPLICATION
BESIEGER	FRAILTY	OUTCAST	REGICIDE	VENERATE
BRAZEN	GROUNDLESS	PARRICIDE	RENOWN	VIGIL
BROOCHES	HARROWED	PARRY	SCANT	VOID
CONTAGION	HEARTH	PASTURAGE	SEPULCHRE	WRETCHED
DECREPIT	HELMSMAN	PERQUISITES	SHROUD	

Oedipus Vocabulary Crossword 1

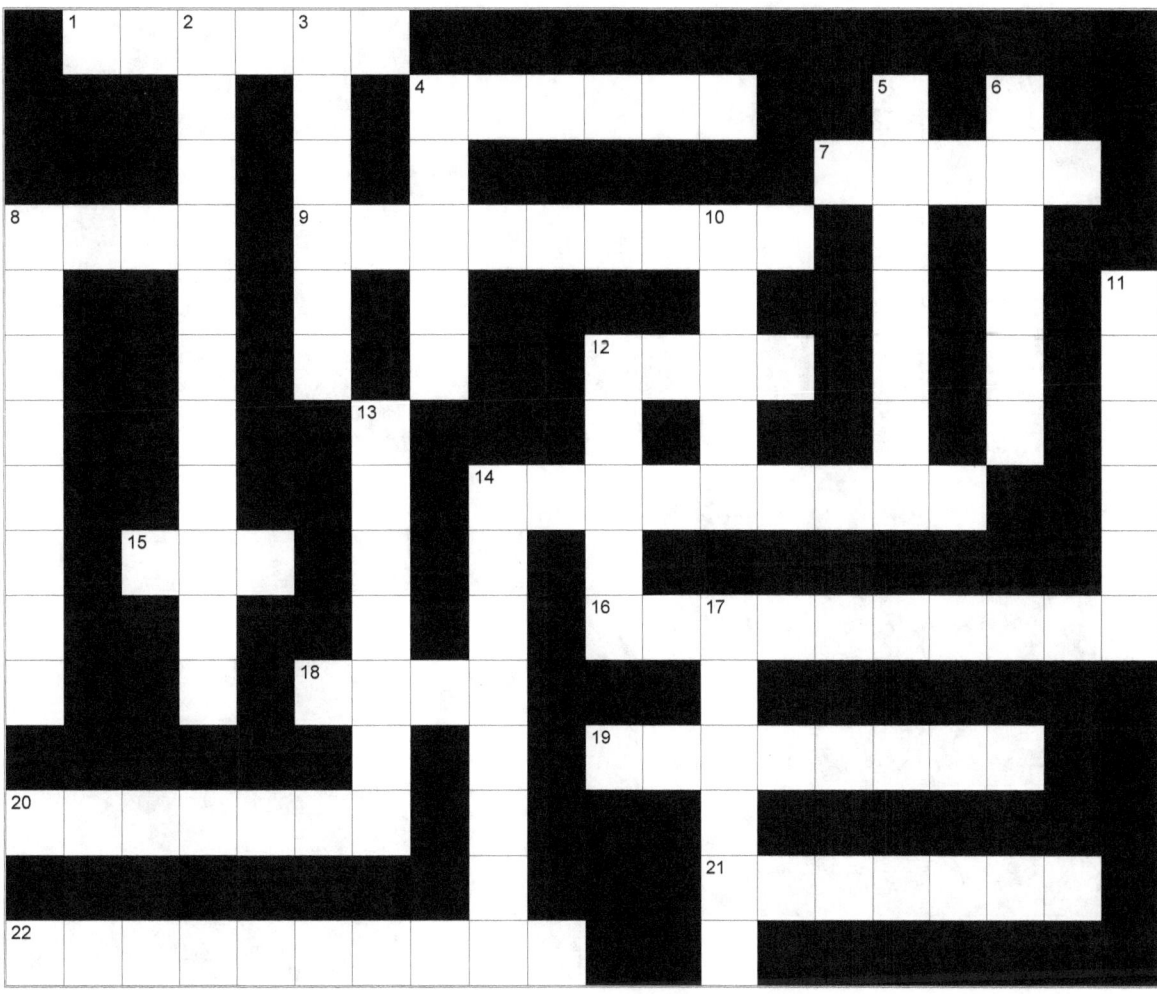

Across
1. Female spirits who lived in forests, bodies of water, and other places outdoors
4. A father's children
7. To turn aside; evade or dodge
8. Freedom from difficulty or great effort
9. Restored confidence to
12. An empty space; emptiness
14. Fathering; siring
15. A loud, disturbing noise
16. The act of purifying by means of ceremony
18. A person or thing that ruins or spoils
19. A person who steers a ship
20. Wise or judicious in practical affairs
21. Any performance or ceremony regarded as absurd or false
22. Without rational basis

Down
2. The utterance of a curse
3. The floor of a fireplace, usually of stone or brick
4. To treat slightly or inadequately
5. A group or clique within a larger group, party, or government
6. Being first in time; original
8. Forced or drove out
10. Any authoritative proclamation or command
11. Widespread and high repute; fame
12. A period of watchful attention maintained at night
13. One who is rejected or discarded
14. Characteristic of or befitting an inferior person or thing
17. Causing serious thoughts or a grave mood

Oedipus Vocabulary Crossword 1 Answer Key

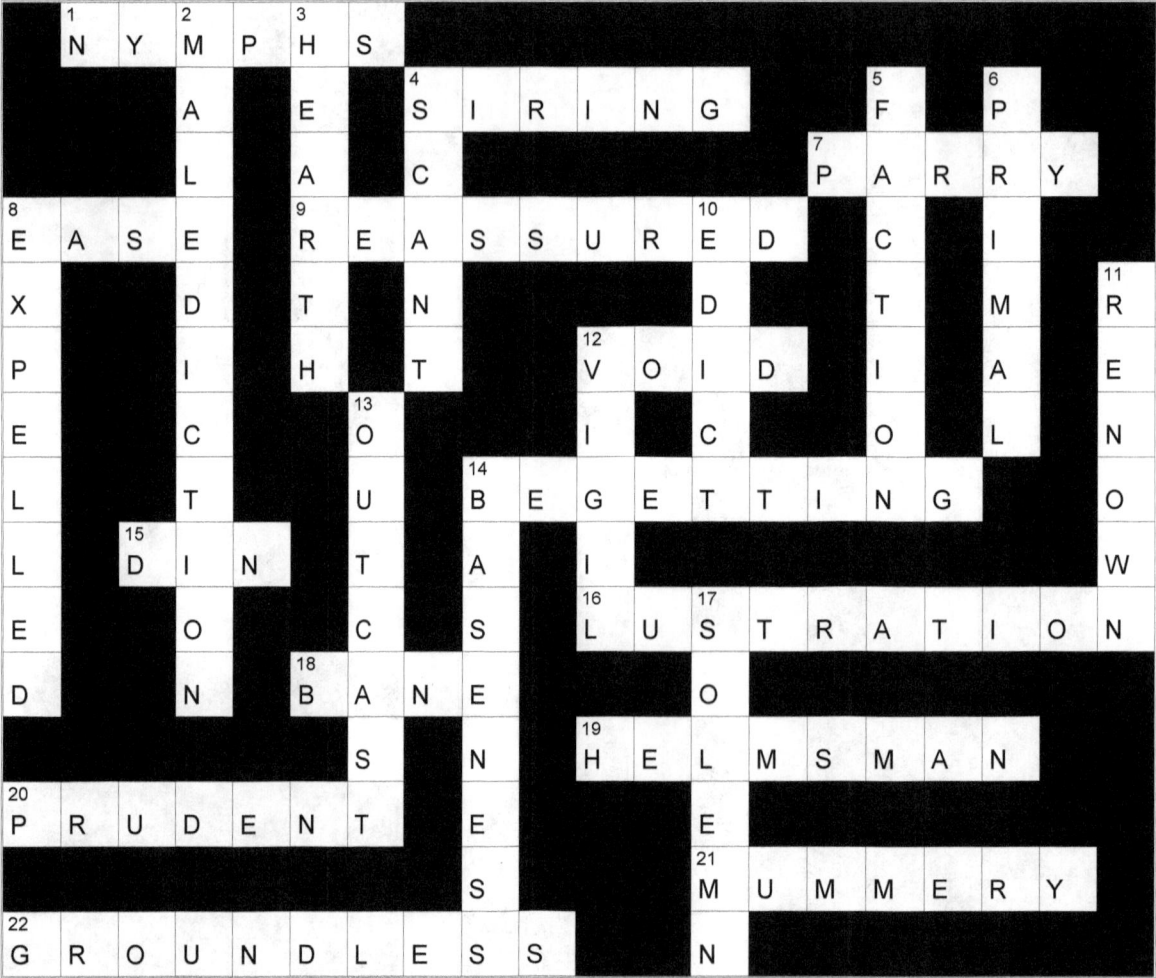

Across
1. Female spirits who lived in forests, bodies of water, and other places outdoors
4. A father's children
7. To turn aside; evade or dodge
8. Freedom from difficulty or great effort
9. Restored confidence to
12. An empty space; emptiness
14. Fathering; siring
15. A loud, disturbing noise
16. The act of purifying by means of ceremony
18. A person or thing that ruins or spoils
19. A person who steers a ship
20. Wise or judicious in practical affairs
21. Any performance or ceremony regarded as absurd or false
22. Without rational basis

Down
2. The utterance of a curse
3. The floor of a fireplace, usually of stone or brick
4. To treat slightly or inadequately
5. A group or clique within a larger group, party, or government
6. Being first in time; original
8. Forced or drove out
10. Any authoritative proclamation or command
11. Widespread and high repute; fame
12. A period of watchful attention maintained at night
13. One who is rejected or discarded
14. Characteristic of or befitting an inferior person or thing
17. Causing serious thoughts or a grave mood

Oedipus Vocabulary Crossword 2

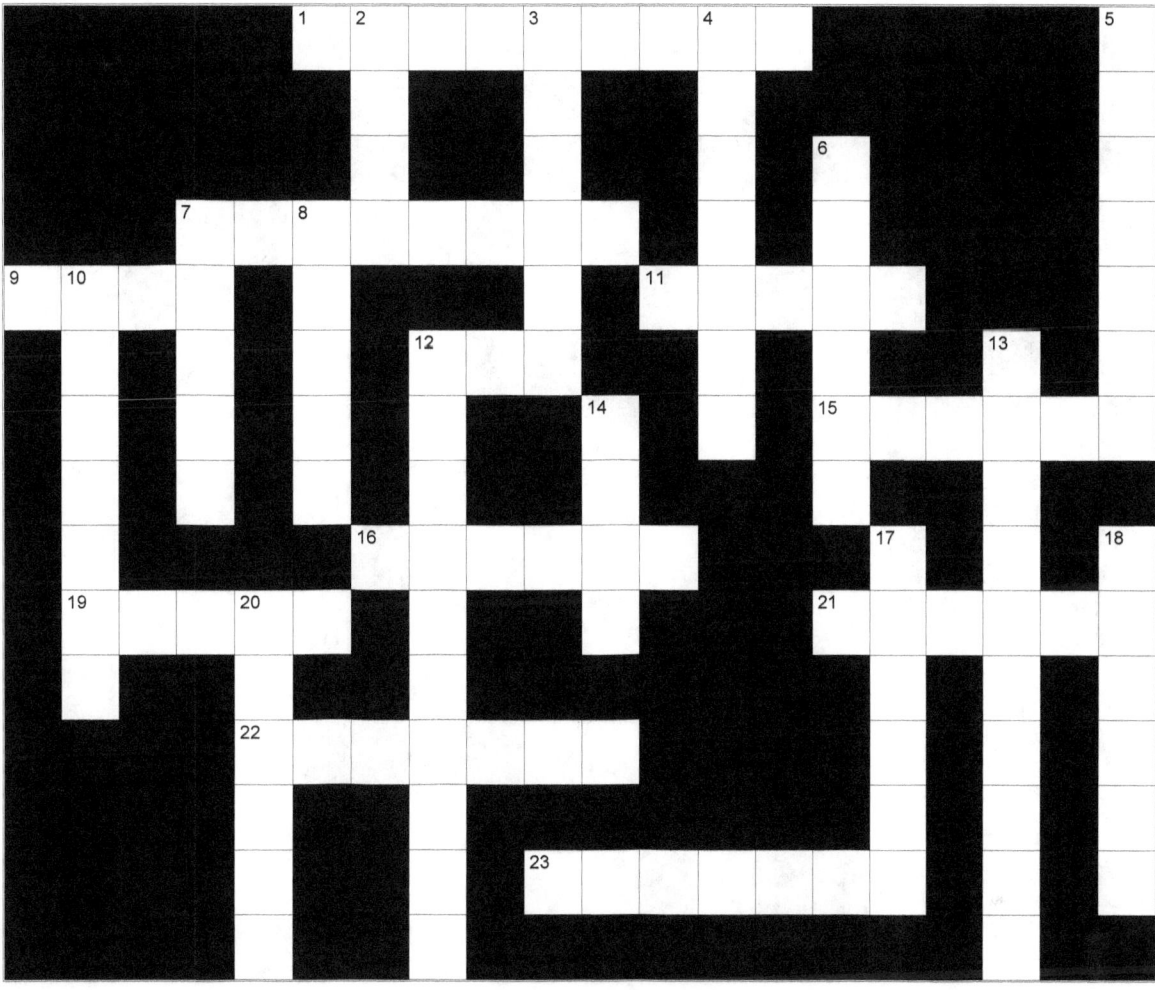

Across
1. Restored confidence to
7. Forced or drove out
9. An empty space; emptiness
11. A period of watchful attention maintained at night
12. A loud, disturbing noise
15. An event indicating important things to come: fortune telling
16. A father's children
19. To treat slightly or inadequately
21. The floor of a fireplace, usually of stone or brick
22. Any performance or ceremony regarded as absurd or false
23. A group or clique within a larger group, party, or government

Down
2. Freedom from difficulty or great effort
3. Causing serious thoughts or a grave mood
4. A seeking or request for truth, information, or knowledge
5. Moral weakness; liability to yield to temptation
6. Being first in time; original
7. Any authoritative proclamation or command
8. To turn aside; evade or dodge
10. One who is rejected or discarded
12. To make foul, dirty, or unclean; pollute
13. The act of purifying by means of ceremony
14. A person or thing that ruins or spoils
17. Widespread and high repute; fame
18. A cloth or sheet in which a corpse is wrapped for burial
20. Female spirits who lived in forests, bodies of water, and other places outdoors

Oedipus Vocabulary Crossword 2 Answer Key

Across
1. Restored confidence to
7. Forced or drove out
9. An empty space; emptiness
11. A period of watchful attention maintained at night
12. A loud, disturbing noise
15. An event indicating important things to come: fortune telling
16. A father's children
19. To treat slightly or inadequately
21. The floor of a fireplace, usually of stone or brick
22. Any performance or ceremony regarded as absurd or false
23. A group or clique within a larger group, party, or government

Down
2. Freedom from difficulty or great effort
3. Causing serious thoughts or a grave mood
4. A seeking or request for truth, information, or knowledge
5. Moral weakness; liability to yield to temptation
6. Being first in time; original
7. Any authoritative proclamation or command
8. To turn aside; evade or dodge
10. One who is rejected or discarded
12. To make foul, dirty, or unclean; pollute
13. The act of purifying by means of ceremony
14. A person or thing that ruins or spoils
17. Widespread and high repute; fame
18. A cloth or sheet in which a corpse is wrapped for burial
20. Female spirits who lived in forests, bodies of water, and other places outdoors

Oedipus Vocabulary Crossword 3

Across
1. To make foul, dirty, or unclean; pollute
3. To turn aside; evade or dodge
4. To take for granted, assume, or suppose
7. A person who kills his own parent
8. An empty space; emptiness
9. To ask for humbly or earnestly, as by praying
12. Female spirits who lived in forests, bodies of water, and other places outdoors
14. Freedom from difficulty or great effort
16. A loud, disturbing noise
18. Any authoritative proclamation or command
19. A person or thing that ruins or spoils
20. Being first in time; original
21. Caused keen irritation or bitter resentment
22. Widespread and high repute; fame

Down
1. Weakened by old age; feeble
2. Relatively large decorative pins or clasps
4. Something that is considered harmful, destructive, or evil
5. To treat slightly or inadequately
6. Moving or acting in an aimless or vague manner
7. The activity or business of pasturing livestock
10. Someone who releases people from captivity or bondage
11. Any uneasiness or hesitation about the rightness of an action
13. The utterance of a curse
15. Causing serious thoughts or a grave mood
17. A period of watchful attention maintained at night

Oedipus Vocabulary Crossword 3 Answer Key

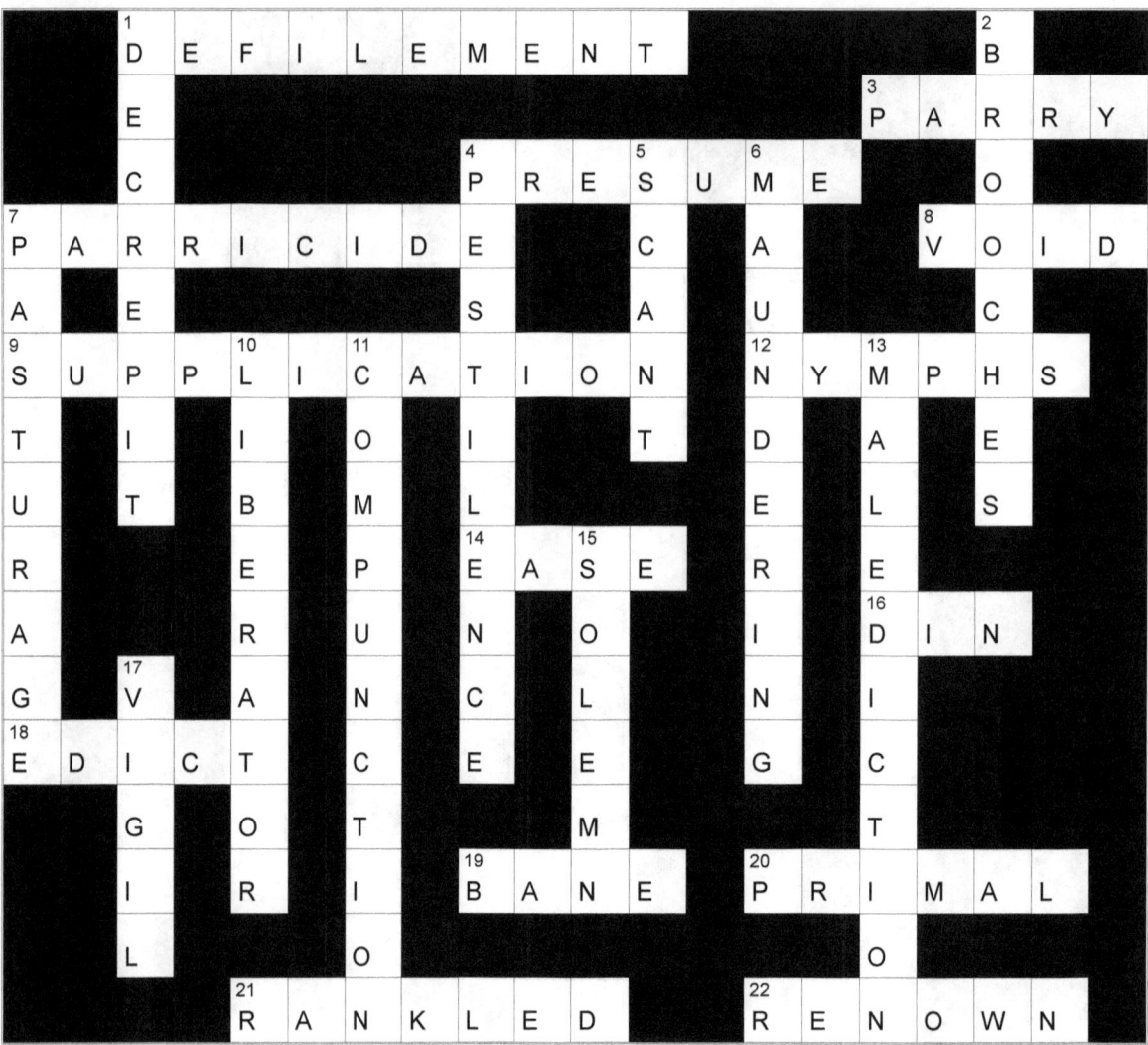

Across
1. To make foul, dirty, or unclean; pollute
3. To turn aside; evade or dodge
4. To take for granted, assume, or suppose
7. A person who kills his own parent
8. An empty space; emptiness
9. To ask for humbly or earnestly, as by praying
12. Female spirits who lived in forests, bodies of water, and other places outdoors
14. Freedom from difficulty or great effort
16. A loud, disturbing noise
18. Any authoritative proclamation or command
19. A person or thing that ruins or spoils
20. Being first in time; original
21. Caused keen irritation or bitter resentment
22. Widespread and high repute; fame

Down
1. Weakened by old age; feeble
2. Relatively large decorative pins or clasps
4. Something that is considered harmful, destructive, or evil
5. To treat slightly or inadequately
6. Moving or acting in an aimless or vague manner
7. The activity or business of pasturing livestock
10. Someone who releases people from captivity or bondage
11. Any uneasiness or hesitation about the rightness of an action
13. The utterance of a curse
15. Causing serious thoughts or a grave mood
17. A period of watchful attention maintained at night

Oedipus Vocabulary Crossword 4

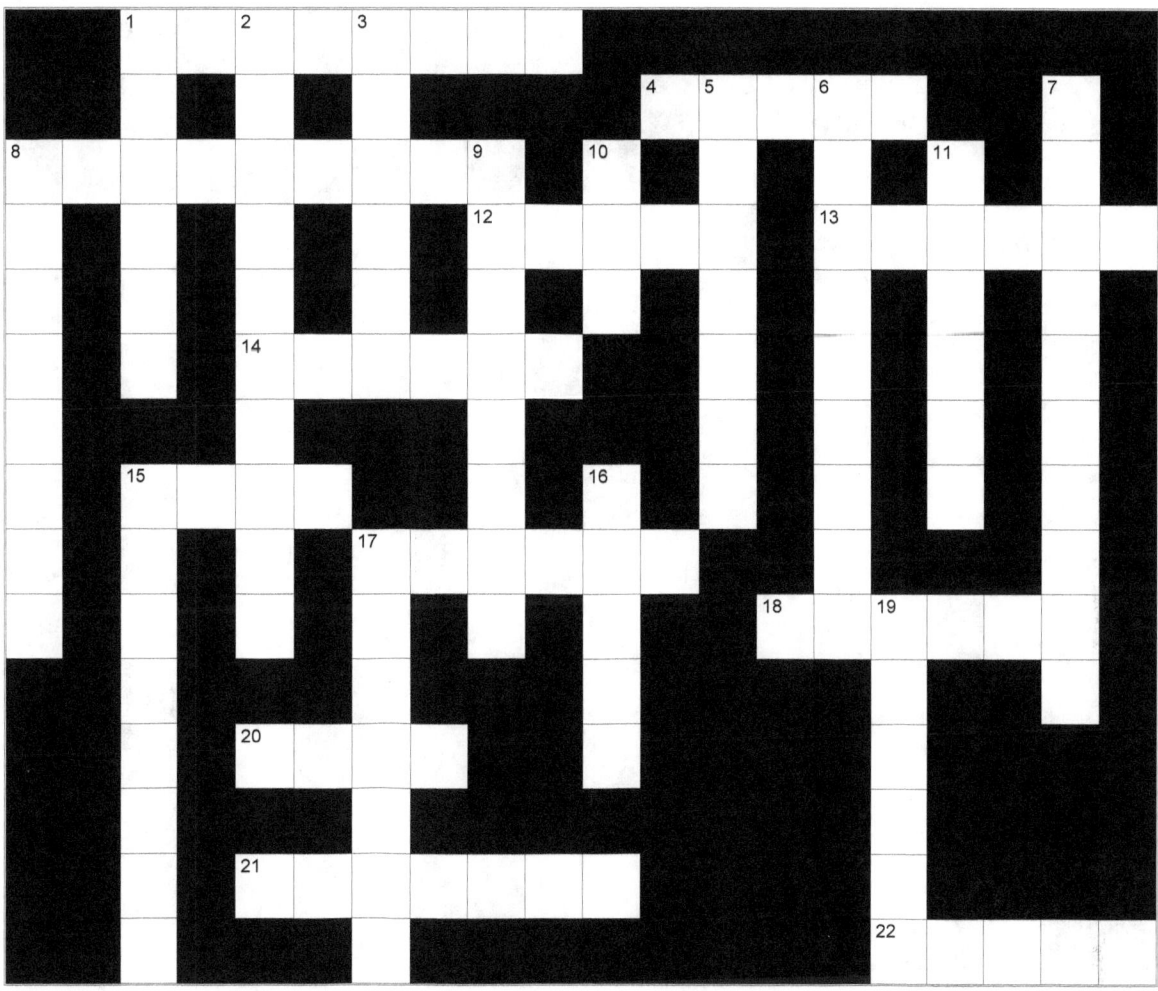

Across
1. A person who steers a ship
4. A period of watchful attention maintained at night
8. Restored confidence to
12. Any authoritative proclamation or command
13. A cloth or sheet in which a corpse is wrapped for burial
14. An event indicating important things to come: fortune telling
15. An empty space; emptiness
17. Being first in time; original
18. Widespread and high repute; fame
20. Freedom from difficulty or great effort
21. Any performance or ceremony regarded as absurd or false
22. To treat slightly or inadequately

Down
1. The floor of a fireplace, usually of stone or brick
2. The act of purifying by means of ceremony
3. A father's children
5. A narrow strip of land, bordered on both sides by water, connecting two larger bodies of land
6. Rude or impertinent behavior or speech
7. Moving or acting in an aimless or vague manner
8. The killing of a king
9. Weakened by old age; feeble
10. A loud, disturbing noise
11. Boldly shameless or impudent
15. To regard or treat with reverence or respect
16. To turn aside; evade or dodge
17. To take for granted, assume, or suppose
19. Female spirits who lived in forests, bodies of water, and other places outdoors

Oedipus Vocabulary Crossword 4 Answer Key

Across
1. A person who steers a ship
4. A period of watchful attention maintained at night
8. Restored confidence to
12. Any authoritative proclamation or command
13. A cloth or sheet in which a corpse is wrapped for burial
14. An event indicating important things to come: fortune telling
15. An empty space; emptiness
17. Being first in time; original
18. Widespread and high repute; fame
20. Freedom from difficulty or great effort
21. Any performance or ceremony regarded as absurd or false
22. To treat slightly or inadequately

Down
1. The floor of a fireplace, usually of stone or brick
2. The act of purifying by means of ceremony
3. A father's children
5. A narrow strip of land, bordered on both sides by water, connecting two larger bodies of land
6. Rude or impertinent behavior or speech
7. Moving or acting in an aimless or vague manner
8. The killing of a king
9. Weakened by old age; feeble
10. A loud, disturbing noise
11. Boldly shameless or impudent
15. To regard or treat with reverence or respect
16. To turn aside; evade or dodge
17. To take for granted, assume, or suppose
19. Female spirits who lived in forests, bodies of water, and other places outdoors

Oedipus Vocabulary Juggle Letters 1

1. HARWODRE = 1. _____
   To break up soil with a toll consisting of a heavy frame with sharp teeth

2. URISQPEETSI = 2. _____
   Those things claimed as exclusive rights

3. TSMSHIU = 3. _____
   A narrow strip of land, bordered on both sides by water, connecting two larger bodies of land

4. YINREQU = 4. _____
   A seeking or request for truth, information, or knowledge

5. RTWGHRVOOEU = 5. _____
   Extremely or excessively excited or agitated

6. AHTEHR = 6. _____
   The floor of a fireplace, usually of stone or brick

7. TNNGCOIOA = 7. _____
   The means by which a contagious disease is transmitted

8. APMRLI = 8. _____
   Being first in time; original

9. CTNSA = 9. _____
   To treat slightly or inadequately

10. TENEFDLMIE =10. _____
    To make foul, dirty, or unclean; pollute

11. RCRPIAIED =11. _____
    A person who kills his own parent

12. EPTENSCILE =12. _____
    Something that is considered harmful, destructive, or evil

13. IGNBTETEG =13. _____
    Fathering; siring

14. OTFCAIN =14. _____
    A group or clique within a larger group, party, or government

Copyrighted

Oedipus Vocabulary Juggle Letters 1 Answer Key

1. HARWODRE = 1. HARROWED
   To break up soil with a toll consisting of a heavy frame with sharp teeth

2. URISQPEETSI = 2. PERQUISITES
   Those things claimed as exclusive rights

3. TSMSHIU = 3. ISTHMUS
   A narrow strip of land, bordered on both sides by water, connecting two larger bodies of land

4. YINREQU = 4. ENQUIRY
   A seeking or request for truth, information, or knowledge

5. RTWGHRVOOEU = 5. OVERWROUGHT
   Extremely or excessively excited or agitated

6. AHTEHR = 6. HEARTH
   The floor of a fireplace, usually of stone or brick

7. TNNGCOIOA = 7. CONTAGION
   The means by which a contagious disease is transmitted

8. APMRLI = 8. PRIMAL
   Being first in time; original

9. CTNSA = 9. SCANT
   To treat slightly or inadequately

10. TENEFDLMIE = 10. DEFILEMENT
    To make foul, dirty, or unclean; pollute

11. RCRPIAIED = 11. PARRICIDE
    A person who kills his own parent

12. EPTENSCILE = 12. PESTILENCE
    Something that is considered harmful, destructive, or evil

13. IGNBTETEG = 13. BEGETTING
    Fathering; siring

14. OTFCAIN = 14. FACTION
    A group or clique within a larger group, party, or government

Oedipus Vocabulary Juggle Letters 2

1. LELDXEPE = 1. _____
   Forced or drove out

2. PARASTUEG = 2. _____
   The activity or business of pasturing livestock

3. MRMEUYM = 3. _____
   Any performance or ceremony regarded as absurd or false

4. GETGNITEB = 4. _____
   Fathering; siring

5. UUYGAR = 5. _____
   An event indicating important things to come: fortune telling

6. IOANITBNMOA = 6. _____
   Anything greatly disliked or abhorred

7. LIPSEENECT = 7. _____
   Something that is considered harmful, destructive, or evil

8. ESSRGULODN = 8. _____
   Without rational basis

9. AEES = 9. _____
   Freedom from difficulty or great effort

10. ROELSPDN =10. _____
    Brilliant or gorgeous appearance

11. DOSUHR =11. _____
    A cloth or sheet in which a corpse is wrapped for burial

12. EIPRCTDE =12. _____
    Weakened by old age; feeble

13. EYSOSRTHOA =13. _____
    Person who professes to foretell events, fortune-teller

14. ATENRVEE =14. _____
    To regard or treat with reverence or respect

Oedipus Vocabulary Juggle Letters 2 Answer Key

1. LELDXEPE = 1. EXPELLED
   Forced or drove out

2. PARASTUEG = 2. PASTURAGE
   The activity or business of pasturing livestock

3. MRMEUYM = 3. MUMMERY
   Any performance or ceremony regarded as absurd or false

4. GETGNITEB = 4. BEGETTING
   Fathering; siring

5. UUYGAR = 5. AUGURY
   An event indicating important things to come: fortune telling

6. IOANITBNMOA = 6. ABOMINATION
   Anything greatly disliked or abhorred

7. LIPSEENECT = 7. PESTILENCE
   Something that is considered harmful, destructive, or evil

8. ESSRGULODN = 8. GROUNDLESS
   Without rational basis

9. AEES = 9. EASE
   Freedom from difficulty or great effort

10. ROELSPDN = 10. SPLENDOR
    Brilliant or gorgeous appearance

11. DOSUHR = 11. SHROUD
    A cloth or sheet in which a corpse is wrapped for burial

12. EIPRCTDE = 12. DECREPIT
    Weakened by old age; feeble

13. EYSOSRTHOA = 13. SOOTHSAYER
    Person who professes to foretell events, fortune-teller

14. ATENRVEE = 14. VENERATE
    To regard or treat with reverence or respect

Oedipus Vocabulary Juggle Letters 3

1. ISIRQPUTESE = 1. _____
   Those things claimed as exclusive rights

2. CDARIRIPE = 2. _____
   A person who kills his own parent

3. AETTBNS = 3. _____
   To thrive and prosper, especially at another's expense

4. PNMHYS = 4. _____
   Female spirits who lived in forests, bodies of water, and other places outdoors

5. HRWDCEET = 5. _____
   Very unfortunate in condition or circumstances

6. RGISNI = 6. _____
   A father's children

7. AECBLXEER = 7. _____
   Utterly detestable; abominable; very bad

8. RUOHDS = 8. _____
   A cloth or sheet in which a corpse is wrapped for burial

9. TREAHH = 9. _____
   The floor of a fireplace, usually of stone or brick

10. AMRLPI = 10. _____
    Being first in time; original

11. EERIGCID = 11. _____
    The killing of a king

12. LDEPLEEX = 12. _____
    Forced or drove out

13. NDI = 13. _____
    A loud, disturbing noise

14. TEDCI = 14. _____
    Any authoritative proclamation or command

Oedipus Vocabulary Juggle Letters 3 Answer Key

1. ISIRQPUTESE = 1. PERQUISITES
   Those things claimed as exclusive rights

2. CDARIRIPE = 2. PARRICIDE
   A person who kills his own parent

3. AETTBNS = 3. BATTENS
   To thrive and prosper, especially at another's expense

4. PNMHYS = 4. NYMPHS
   Female spirits who lived in forests, bodies of water, and other places outdoors

5. HRWDCEET = 5. WRETCHED
   Very unfortunate in condition or circumstances

6. RGISNI = 6. SIRING
   A father's children

7. AECBLXEER = 7. EXECRABLE
   Utterly detestable; abominable; very bad

8. RUOHDS = 8. SHROUD
   A cloth or sheet in which a corpse is wrapped for burial

9. TREAHH = 9. HEARTH
   The floor of a fireplace, usually of stone or brick

10. AMRLPI =10. PRIMAL
    Being first in time; original

11. EERIGCID =11. REGICIDE
    The killing of a king

12. LDEPLEEX =12. EXPELLED
    Forced or drove out

13. NDI =13. DIN
    A loud, disturbing noise

14. TEDCI =14. EDICT
    Any authoritative proclamation or command

Oedipus Vocabulary Juggle Letters 4

1. CEEILTNSEP = 1. _____
   Something that is considered harmful, destructive, or evil

2. GURUAY = 2. _____
   An event indicating important things to come: fortune telling

3. SBENSEAS = 3. _____
   Characteristic of or befitting an inferior person or thing

4. LXEEELDP = 4. _____
   Forced or drove out

5. ERSTHYOOSA = 5. _____
   Person who professes to foretell events, fortune-teller

6. OWRNNE = 6. _____
   Widespread and high repute; fame

7. EBZRAN = 7. _____
   Boldly shameless or impudent

8. YQRUNIE = 8. _____
   A seeking or request for truth, information, or knowledge

9. ICNUAPISLPTO = 9. _____
   To ask for humbly or earnestly, as by praying

10. AEHLSNMM = 10. _____
    A person who steers a ship

11. LUTPSPANI = 11. _____
    One who asks humbly and earnestly

12. HUTSMSI = 12. _____
    A narrow strip of land, bordered on both sides by water, connecting two larger bodies of land

13. CDETI = 13. _____
    Any authoritative proclamation or command

14. NPUTDER = 14. _____
    Wise or judicious in practical affairs

Oedipus Vocabulary Juggle Letters 4 Answer Key

1. CEEILTNSEP = 1. PESTILENCE
   Something that is considered harmful, destructive, or evil

2. GURUAY = 2. AUGURY
   An event indicating important things to come: fortune telling

3. SBENSEAS = 3. BASENESS
   Characteristic of or befitting an inferior person or thing

4. LXEEELDP = 4. EXPELLED
   Forced or drove out

5. ERSTHYOOSA = 5. SOOTHSAYER
   Person who professes to foretell events, fortune-teller

6. OWRNNE = 6. RENOWN
   Widespread and high repute; fame

7. EBZRAN = 7. BRAZEN
   Boldly shameless or impudent

8. YQRUNIE = 8. ENQUIRY
   A seeking or request for truth, information, or knowledge

9. ICNUAPISLPTO = 9. SUPPLICATION
   To ask for humbly or earnestly, as by praying

10. AEHLSNMM = 10. HELMSMAN
    A person who steers a ship

11. LUTPSPANI = 11. SUPPLIANT
    One who asks humbly and earnestly

12. HUTSMSI = 12. ISTHMUS
    A narrow strip of land, bordered on both sides by water, connecting two larger bodies of land

13. CDETI = 13. EDICT
    Any authoritative proclamation or command

14. NPUTDER = 14. PRUDENT
    Wise or judicious in practical affairs

ABOMINATION	Anything greatly disliked or abhorred
AUGURY	An event indicating important things to come: fortune telling
BANE	A person or thing that ruins or spoils
BASENESS	Characteristic of or befitting an inferior person or thing
BATTENS	To thrive and prosper, especially at another's expense

BEGETTING	Fathering; siring
BESIEGER	An enemy who lays siege to your positions
BRAZEN	Boldly shameless or impudent
BROOCHES	Relatively large decorative pins or clasps
COMPUNCTION	Any uneasiness or hesitation about the rightness of an action

CONTAGION	The means by which a contagious disease is transmitted
DECREPIT	Weakened by old age; feeble
DEFILEMENT	To make foul, dirty, or unclean; pollute
DIN	A loud, disturbing noise
EASE	Freedom from difficulty or great effort

EDICT	Any authoritative proclamation or command
ENQUIRY	A seeking or request for truth, information, or knowledge
EXECRABLE	Utterly detestable; abominable; very bad
EXPELLED	Forced or drove out
FACTION	A group or clique within a larger group, party, or government

FRAILTY	Moral weakness; liability to yield to temptation
GROUNDLESS	Without rational basis
HARROWED	To break up soil with a toll consisting of a heavy frame with sharp teeth
HEARTH	The floor of a fireplace, usually of stone or brick
HELMSMAN	A person who steers a ship

INSOLENCE	Rude or impertinent behavior or speech
ISTHMUS	A narrow strip of land, bordered on both sides by water, connecting two larger bodies of land
LIBERATOR	Someone who releases people from captivity or bondage
LUSTRATION	The act of purifying by means of ceremony
MALEDICTION	The utterance of a curse

MAUNDERING	Moving or acting in an aimless or vague manner
MUMMERY	Any performance or ceremony regarded as absurd or false
NYMPHS	Female spirits who lived in forests, bodies of water, and other places outdoors
OUTCAST	One who is rejected or discarded
OVERWROUGHT	Extremely or excessively excited or agitated

PARRICIDE	A person who kills his own parent
PARRY	To turn aside; evade or dodge
PASTURAGE	The activity or business of pasturing livestock
PERQUISITES	Those things claimed as exclusive rights
PESTILENCE	Something that is considered harmful, destructive, or evil

PRESUME	To take for granted, assume, or suppose
PRIMAL	Being first in time; original
PRUDENT	Wise or judicious in practical affairs
RANKLED	Caused keen irritation or bitter resentment
REASSURED	Restored confidence to

REGICIDE	The killing of a king
RENOWN	Widespread and high repute; fame
SCANT	To treat slightly or inadequately
SEPULCHRE	A tomb, grave, or burial place
SHROUD	A cloth or sheet in which a corpse is wrapped for burial

SIRING	A father's children
SOLEMN	Causing serious thoughts or a grave mood
SOOTHSAYER	Person who professes to foretell events, fortune-teller
SPLENDOR	Brilliant or gorgeous appearance
SUPPLIANT	One who asks humbly and earnestly

SUPPLICATION	To ask for humbly or earnestly, as by praying
VENERATE	To regard or treat with reverence or respect
VIGIL	A period of watchful attention maintained at night
VOID	An empty space; emptiness
WRETCHED	Very unfortunate in condition or circumstances

Oedipus Vocabulary

FACTION	DEFILEMENT	PARRY	PERQUISITES	MAUNDERING
SCANT	BRAZEN	HELMSMAN	CONTAGION	EXPELLED
ISTHMUS	LIBERATOR	FREE SPACE	REGICIDE	HEARTH
BATTENS	ABOMINATION	SOOTHSAYER	VIGIL	SPLENDOR
EXECRABLE	REASSURED	VENERATE	EASE	BANE

Oedipus Vocabulary

SUPPLIANT	SIRING	WRETCHED	DECREPIT	BASENESS
MALEDICTION	OUTCAST	EDICT	PRESUME	NYMPHS
GROUNDLESS	BEGETTING	FREE SPACE	RENOWN	COMPUNCTION
ENQUIRY	DIN	RANKLED	SOLEMN	PRIMAL
SUPPLICATION	OVERWROUGHT	SHROUD	AUGURY	SEPULCHRE

Oedipus Vocabulary

PARRY	EXPELLED	REASSURED	OUTCAST	REGICIDE
OVERWROUGHT	BASENESS	HELMSMAN	SOOTHSAYER	SIRING
CONTAGION	VENERATE	FREE SPACE	EDICT	INSOLENCE
MAUNDERING	DEFILEMENT	VOID	SPLENDOR	BESIEGER
DECREPIT	WRETCHED	SEPULCHRE	AUGURY	BROOCHES

Oedipus Vocabulary

NYMPHS	HEARTH	MALEDICTION	SUPPLIANT	ISTHMUS
PESTILENCE	VIGIL	COMPUNCTION	ABOMINATION	HARROWED
SUPPLICATION	FRAILTY	FREE SPACE	BRAZEN	SOLEMN
EASE	BATTENS	PARRICIDE	SCANT	GROUNDLESS
PASTURAGE	MUMMERY	LIBERATOR	PRUDENT	RENOWN

Oedipus Vocabulary

DEFILEMENT	VIGIL	OVERWROUGHT	HEARTH	SEPULCHRE
PARRICIDE	FRAILTY	ENQUIRY	VENERATE	BEGETTING
PRIMAL	PESTILENCE	FREE SPACE	EXECRABLE	PRESUME
RANKLED	SCANT	BROOCHES	MAUNDERING	BATTENS
GROUNDLESS	EDICT	DIN	SOOTHSAYER	MUMMERY

Oedipus Vocabulary

ISTHMUS	WRETCHED	EXPELLED	BANE	BRAZEN
PASTURAGE	REGICIDE	LUSTRATION	PARRY	DECREPIT
PERQUISITES	EASE	FREE SPACE	PRUDENT	SUPPLICATION
BESIEGER	SUPPLIANT	SIRING	BASENESS	COMPUNCTION
REASSURED	OUTCAST	HARROWED	AUGURY	SHROUD

Oedipus Vocabulary

HEARTH	EXECRABLE	BASENESS	BRAZEN	FACTION
EDICT	PARRY	SCANT	RENOWN	BEGETTING
OVERWROUGHT	AUGURY	FREE SPACE	SHROUD	PRIMAL
VIGIL	SOOTHSAYER	MUMMERY	BANE	BESIEGER
LIBERATOR	DIN	BROOCHES	GROUNDLESS	SPLENDOR

Oedipus Vocabulary

FRAILTY	CONTAGION	SIRING	REGICIDE	INSOLENCE
OUTCAST	HELMSMAN	PRUDENT	MAUNDERING	ISTHMUS
NYMPHS	MALEDICTION	FREE SPACE	SUPPLICATION	PARRICIDE
RANKLED	COMPUNCTION	SOLEMN	SEPULCHRE	DECREPIT
EASE	SUPPLIANT	PERQUISITES	VOID	LUSTRATION

Oedipus Vocabulary

PASTURAGE	SOOTHSAYER	VIGIL	SHROUD	DIN
REASSURED	RENOWN	EASE	OUTCAST	ISTHMUS
SOLEMN	BEGETTING	FREE SPACE	EXPELLED	AUGURY
COMPUNCTION	WRETCHED	PRIMAL	PRESUME	SUPPLICATION
HELMSMAN	HEARTH	BANE	FRAILTY	SPLENDOR

Oedipus Vocabulary

OVERWROUGHT	ENQUIRY	SEPULCHRE	MAUNDERING	PESTILENCE
ABOMINATION	MALEDICTION	HARROWED	BATTENS	LIBERATOR
VOID	BRAZEN	FREE SPACE	RANKLED	INSOLENCE
EXECRABLE	BASENESS	SUPPLIANT	SCANT	BROOCHES
GROUNDLESS	CONTAGION	DECREPIT	LUSTRATION	FACTION

Oedipus Vocabulary

RANKLED	RENOWN	SCANT	OUTCAST	BANE
SUPPLICATION	HELMSMAN	PRESUME	BESIEGER	SOOTHSAYER
PRUDENT	SPLENDOR	FREE SPACE	VIGIL	EDICT
LIBERATOR	CONTAGION	EASE	EXECRABLE	FRAILTY
REGICIDE	VOID	SHROUD	HEARTH	COMPUNCTION

Oedipus Vocabulary

BATTENS	WRETCHED	MUMMERY	EXPELLED	DECREPIT
ABOMINATION	BASENESS	LUSTRATION	PRIMAL	SOLEMN
AUGURY	FACTION	FREE SPACE	VENERATE	SUPPLIANT
DEFILEMENT	HARROWED	BRAZEN	BROOCHES	ENQUIRY
MAUNDERING	BEGETTING	PARRY	OVERWROUGHT	INSOLENCE

Oedipus Vocabulary

BROOCHES	HARROWED	SHROUD	GROUNDLESS	INSOLENCE
MAUNDERING	RENOWN	EASE	BASENESS	SCANT
ISTHMUS	MUMMERY	FREE SPACE	WRETCHED	NYMPHS
RANKLED	BESIEGER	LIBERATOR	REASSURED	PESTILENCE
REGICIDE	COMPUNCTION	LUSTRATION	DECREPIT	MALEDICTION

Oedipus Vocabulary

PARRY	BANE	OVERWROUGHT	PRUDENT	PARRICIDE
VENERATE	HELMSMAN	PRESUME	CONTAGION	ABOMINATION
BEGETTING	EXPELLED	FREE SPACE	SOOTHSAYER	PASTURAGE
SUPPLICATION	DEFILEMENT	FACTION	FRAILTY	BATTENS
OUTCAST	VOID	SEPULCHRE	SOLEMN	PRIMAL

Oedipus Vocabulary

PARRY	AUGURY	EASE	FRAILTY	SUPPLICATION
VOID	BROOCHES	EXECRABLE	FACTION	VENERATE
REASSURED	BASENESS	FREE SPACE	PRUDENT	PARRICIDE
REGICIDE	PESTILENCE	DECREPIT	NYMPHS	BRAZEN
BATTENS	CONTAGION	RENOWN	OUTCAST	SIRING

Oedipus Vocabulary

MUMMERY	MALEDICTION	SHROUD	GROUNDLESS	VIGIL
BEGETTING	SOOTHSAYER	HEARTH	BESIEGER	OVERWROUGHT
EDICT	SEPULCHRE	FREE SPACE	PASTURAGE	HELMSMAN
SCANT	LUSTRATION	ENQUIRY	DIN	RANKLED
WRETCHED	PERQUISITES	DEFILEMENT	COMPUNCTION	SOLEMN

Oedipus Vocabulary

EASE	PRESUME	EXPELLED	PARRICIDE	MUMMERY
PARRY	DIN	PESTILENCE	REASSURED	BEGETTING
VENERATE	GROUNDLESS	FREE SPACE	RENOWN	PRIMAL
ENQUIRY	INSOLENCE	HEARTH	SHROUD	BANE
NYMPHS	SEPULCHRE	EXECRABLE	AUGURY	FACTION

Oedipus Vocabulary

SPLENDOR	PASTURAGE	SOOTHSAYER	ABOMINATION	SIRING
EDICT	MALEDICTION	VIGIL	OVERWROUGHT	VOID
BATTENS	FRAILTY	FREE SPACE	OUTCAST	COMPUNCTION
DEFILEMENT	BROOCHES	PERQUISITES	RANKLED	BRAZEN
DECREPIT	BESIEGER	REGICIDE	BASENESS	SUPPLICATION

Oedipus Vocabulary

VIGIL	RENOWN	COMPUNCTION	MALEDICTION	HELMSMAN
FACTION	SUPPLIANT	MUMMERY	PRESUME	BASENESS
VOID	OVERWROUGHT	FREE SPACE	GROUNDLESS	LIBERATOR
BROOCHES	MAUNDERING	BANE	PARRY	PRIMAL
SOLEMN	RANKLED	CONTAGION	DECREPIT	BEGETTING

Oedipus Vocabulary

OUTCAST	ABOMINATION	NYMPHS	SPLENDOR	ISTHMUS
EXECRABLE	BESIEGER	ENQUIRY	WRETCHED	LUSTRATION
BRAZEN	DIN	FREE SPACE	REASSURED	REGICIDE
SEPULCHRE	SUPPLICATION	SHROUD	HEARTH	PERQUISITES
FRAILTY	PASTURAGE	INSOLENCE	VENERATE	BATTENS

Oedipus Vocabulary

SOOTHSAYER	FACTION	EDICT	PASTURAGE	INSOLENCE
HARROWED	VOID	MAUNDERING	PERQUISITES	PRUDENT
EASE	GROUNDLESS	FREE SPACE	BASENESS	REGICIDE
ABOMINATION	EXPELLED	WRETCHED	PRESUME	COMPUNCTION
FRAILTY	BANE	NYMPHS	EXECRABLE	RANKLED

Oedipus Vocabulary

BROOCHES	BESIEGER	ENQUIRY	HEARTH	PESTILENCE
SIRING	PARRICIDE	VENERATE	BEGETTING	REASSURED
AUGURY	MALEDICTION	FREE SPACE	SOLEMN	SHROUD
DIN	LIBERATOR	MUMMERY	VIGIL	SUPPLIANT
CONTAGION	LUSTRATION	PRIMAL	SUPPLICATION	SPLENDOR

Oedipus Vocabulary

SCANT	OVERWROUGHT	PRUDENT	FACTION	PRESUME
LIBERATOR	HELMSMAN	SIRING	CONTAGION	PASTURAGE
BEGETTING	NYMPHS	FREE SPACE	DIN	EXECRABLE
WRETCHED	SOLEMN	VIGIL	RANKLED	ISTHMUS
EASE	INSOLENCE	PESTILENCE	MALEDICTION	BROOCHES

Oedipus Vocabulary

DECREPIT	BRAZEN	SOOTHSAYER	SUPPLIANT	SUPPLICATION
MAUNDERING	FRAILTY	RENOWN	ABOMINATION	REGICIDE
MUMMERY	EXPELLED	FREE SPACE	LUSTRATION	VOID
SPLENDOR	BESIEGER	BANE	COMPUNCTION	BASENESS
REASSURED	BATTENS	GROUNDLESS	PARRY	SHROUD

Oedipus Vocabulary

REASSURED	FRAILTY	SCANT	INSOLENCE	SHROUD
HEARTH	SIRING	RANKLED	PRUDENT	MALEDICTION
PARRY	SEPULCHRE	FREE SPACE	PASTURAGE	PRIMAL
DIN	BROOCHES	WRETCHED	SOLEMN	PESTILENCE
LUSTRATION	HARROWED	NYMPHS	EXECRABLE	ISTHMUS

Oedipus Vocabulary

OVERWROUGHT	RENOWN	SUPPLICATION	EASE	DEFILEMENT
EXPELLED	LIBERATOR	PRESUME	BEGETTING	MAUNDERING
BESIEGER	BRAZEN	FREE SPACE	ENQUIRY	GROUNDLESS
VENERATE	PARRICIDE	SOOTHSAYER	BANE	COMPUNCTION
FACTION	ABOMINATION	BASENESS	SPLENDOR	OUTCAST

Oedipus Vocabulary

MAUNDERING	OVERWROUGHT	HEARTH	PERQUISITES	BEGETTING
VENERATE	OUTCAST	BATTENS	COMPUNCTION	RENOWN
SUPPLIANT	FRAILTY	FREE SPACE	SCANT	SOLEMN
ENQUIRY	VOID	MALEDICTION	LUSTRATION	BROOCHES
DECREPIT	PARRICIDE	SHROUD	PASTURAGE	PRIMAL

Oedipus Vocabulary

ISTHMUS	HELMSMAN	DIN	BESIEGER	EXPELLED
REASSURED	PRUDENT	REGICIDE	GROUNDLESS	EASE
INSOLENCE	MUMMERY	FREE SPACE	SOOTHSAYER	RANKLED
PESTILENCE	EDICT	BASENESS	DEFILEMENT	PRESUME
FACTION	BANE	CONTAGION	EXECRABLE	WRETCHED

Oedipus Vocabulary

PRESUME	PERQUISITES	RANKLED	DECREPIT	BRAZEN
VOID	FRAILTY	INSOLENCE	AUGURY	EDICT
PASTURAGE	REASSURED	FREE SPACE	BEGETTING	WRETCHED
SOLEMN	FACTION	COMPUNCTION	DEFILEMENT	SIRING
PRUDENT	PARRICIDE	LIBERATOR	SCANT	BROOCHES

Oedipus Vocabulary

HEARTH	SPLENDOR	SUPPLICATION	BANE	RENOWN
GROUNDLESS	EXPELLED	EXECRABLE	REGICIDE	PESTILENCE
VENERATE	CONTAGION	FREE SPACE	SOOTHSAYER	SEPULCHRE
NYMPHS	MALEDICTION	HELMSMAN	OUTCAST	PRIMAL
PARRY	BASENESS	ABOMINATION	VIGIL	HARROWED

Oedipus Vocabulary

SHROUD	MUMMERY	EASE	NYMPHS	AUGURY
REGICIDE	PARRICIDE	SEPULCHRE	MAUNDERING	EXECRABLE
ENQUIRY	VIGIL	FREE SPACE	HEARTH	SUPPLIANT
DIN	PRIMAL	BASENESS	HELMSMAN	BESIEGER
ISTHMUS	DECREPIT	RANKLED	INSOLENCE	COMPUNCTION

Oedipus Vocabulary

BEGETTING	OVERWROUGHT	SCANT	BANE	SPLENDOR
OUTCAST	CONTAGION	LUSTRATION	FACTION	VENERATE
HARROWED	WRETCHED	FREE SPACE	VOID	DEFILEMENT
BRAZEN	RENOWN	ABOMINATION	FRAILTY	PERQUISITES
SIRING	SUPPLICATION	MALEDICTION	BROOCHES	PARRY

www.ingramcontent.com/pod-product-compliance
Lightning Source LLC
LaVergne TN
LVHW081537060526
838200LV00048B/2116